Follow the Dog

A History of the St. Paul Police Canine Unit
1958-2008

by
Ruth Gordon

ISBN 13: 978-1-880654-43-9
Library of Congress Control No. 2008923448

Cover image:
Larry Nevin and Duke were involved in the search for Willie Seal, May 1978. Seal, a blind boy aged eleven, wandered off from a school visit to Crosby Lake. Several hundred volunteers, National Guard soldiers, and ten canine/handler teams searched for him. The child's body was eventually recovered from the Mississippi River. Courtesy of the St. Paul Police Department.

Photographic and other credits:
A. J. Forliti Photographer, 67 (all three); Ed Buehlman 17, 18, 19, 20; St. Paul Police Department, 41, 49, 51, 66 (both), 68, 72 (and cover); *St. Paul Pioneer Press*, 37, 59, 60, 78; Larry Nevin, 27, 38, 48; Glen Kothe, 29, 47; Nicole Rasmussen 40; Larry McDonald, 14; American Kennel Club, 8; and Ruth Gordon, 13, 43, 52, 54, 69 and 77.

Cover and chapter backgrounds and borders:
American Flag on Paper © Nic Taylor. Image from istockphotos.com
Old Paper and Stars © Selahattin Bayram. Image from istockphotos.com

Designed by Angela Wix
Edited by Lindsey Cunneen

Published by Pogo Press
An Imprint of Finney Company
8075 215th Street West
Lakeville, Minnesota 55044
www.pogopress.com
www.finneyco.com

Printed in China
1 3 5 7 9 10 8 6 4 2

We are deeply indebted

to John Nasseff
and an anonymous donor
for their generous contributions to this project

Table of Contents

Preface .... *ix*

Introduction .... *xi*

Acknowledgments .... *xiii*

One   The History of Using Dogs in Police Work 1

Two   The First Use of Police Dogs in St. Paul 11

Three   Police Dogs Return to St. Paul 25

Four   Education and Training of the Handlers 35

Five   The Remarkable Dogs 45

Six   Officer Down 57

Seven   Recognition and Awards 65

Eight   The St. Paul Police Canine Unit Today 75

Appendix A: Executive Officers and Head Trainers, 1972–2008 83

Appendix B: 2008 Members of the St. Paul K-9 Police Foundation Board 84

Appendix C: 2008 Officers of the St. Paul Police Historical Society Board 85

Appendix D: 2008 Handlers in the St. Paul Police Canine Unit 86

Index 91

DEPARTMENT OF POLICE
John M. Harrington, Chief of Police

CITY OF SAINT PAUL
Christopher B. Coleman, Mayor

367 Grove Street
Saint Paul, Minnesota 55101

Telephone: 651-291-1111
Facsimile: 651-266-5711

March 7, 2008

Dear Readers:

On behalf of the Saint Paul Police Department, I am honored to introduce you to the book, Follow the Dog: A History of the Saint Paul Police Canine Unit.

Canine officers and their partners are essential to the successful operation of a modern police department. Members of our Canine Unit have not only met the national standards of the United States Police K-9 Association, but they have also distinguished themselves in national competitions and outstanding case awards. Collectively, they have produced five U.S.P.C.A. national team championships, three U.S.P.C.A. national individual patrol dog champions and over three hundred national, regional or Departmental awards for quality police performance.

The Saint Paul Police Canine Unit commenced fifty years ago in 1958. It is one of the oldest canine organizations in the United States. Today we utilize twenty-two (22) police service dog teams and have become the primary agency in the upper Midwest for canine recruitment and training.

It is fitting that this book comes out on the Unit's fiftieth anniversary as well as the sesquicentennial year of the State of Minnesota. This book brings to life the work, the triumphs, and the tragedies of the men and women working with their canine partners.

Sincerely,

John M. Harrington
CHIEF OF POLICE
Saint Paul Police Department

An Affirmative Action Equal Opportunity Employer

Our beloved dog Ben, a golden retriever, gave me a retirement career writing true dog stories. As I found remarkable dogs to write about, my interest in dogs widened. That is why my husband and I found ourselves at the 2002 spring graduation ceremony of the St. Paul Police Canine Unit. We were there because we had the time, love and admire dogs, and we wanted to learn more about the officers and dogs doing canine police work.

The graduating dogs and their partners demonstrated some of the things they had learned to do together: climbing ladders, walking on planks at dizzying heights, attacking bad guys (on command), jumping through car windows when ordered, tracking a scent, and most importantly, demonstrating the strength and stamina it takes to perform these rigorous training exercises. It could hardly have been more impressive.

In the spring of 2006, my husband and I visited the American Kennel Club Museum of the Dog in St. Louis, Missouri. It is adjacent to a lovely old mansion on the beautiful grounds of the city's Queeny Park. In the museum building are: an extensive exhibit of paintings and sculptures of dogs, a case of dog collars through the ages, a gift shop, and a Hall of Fame. The Hall of Fame celebrates dogs from Hollywood films (Lassie, Rin Tin Tin, Toto, and others), the history of War Dogs, and the St. Paul Police Canine Unit, "one of the finest in the United States." Discovering that our local canine unit was so prestigious gave us a nice sense of pride. It also meant that we wanted to get better acquainted with our hometown celebrities. We arrived home just in time to attend the 2006 spring graduation of the St. Paul Police Canine Unit. It was as impressive as we remembered, but they had added one new exciting element. A helicopter landed in the middle of the training grounds and out came a dog with his human partner shooting at a pretend robber. Everyone in the stands jumped when they heard the gun shots, but the sounds did not disturb any of the dogs.

Before leaving the training grounds in Maplewood, I introduced myself to Officer Mark Ficcadenti, the Head Trainer. I needed a story about a dog helping a person for a book I was writing. Mark was good enough to make an appointment with me the following week. Mark naturally had many stories, but I chose to write about some of the times Tyke, his canine partner, either saved Mark's life or helped capture a killer. Tyke was Mark's partner for nine years. Then, as the family pet, Tyke retired with Mark's family and lived to be 13 years old. Some of their experiences as partners became the final story in my book, *Good Dogs: Stories of Benevolence.*

That encounter became the beginning of a new writing project because I discovered that there is a proud history that needed to be told about the work of St Paul's canine unit, which first started fifty years ago. The St. Paul Police Canine Unit has been nationally known for a decade but that is virtually unknown locally. In fact, I discovered that many of the officers in the unit were unaware that the St. Paul unit was prominently featured in the Hall of Fame at the Museum of the Dog in St. Louis, Missouri. It seemed time to record the unit's history.

I am sorry this book is now finished because I will miss listening to the experiences of past and present canine handlers. The stories of courage, hard work, tragedies, successes, and "But don't put that in the book," have made me deeply appreciative of canine police work.

Larry McDonald, now vice president of the St. Paul Police Historical Society Board, shared his personal papers and scrapbooks, and reviewed Chapter Two for me. Ed Buehlman shared his papers and time, and Kate Cavett's oral histories were most helpful.

Larry Nevin brought his photograph album and memories of the unit's early days. Archie Smith and Jim Cocchiarella filled in many blanks about the unit's beginnings.

Thanks to Glen Kothe for the tour of his Total Recall School for Dogs, for sharing his scrapbook, wonderful stories and time, and for reviewing Chapter Three. Tim Lynaugh was willing to tell me about the events leading to Callahan's death. His stories and insights were invaluable.

Sergeant Paul Dunnom gave me access to large boxes of photographs, books, training manuals, and miscellaneous clippings. He made at least a dozen telephone calls to people I wanted to interview. That was critical in gaining access to retired handlers in particular. And he reviewed Chapter Eight.

Officer Mark Ficcadenti opened more doors for me, tracked down dates, and reviewed Chapters Four and Five. His wealth of experience and knowledge of the workings of the unit, both past and present, could not be found anywhere else. And, most of all, I am grateful for so much of his time.

Thanks to Nicole Rasmussen for her perceptive insights and her stunning pictures.

Dave Pavlak worked the computers, gathering hundreds of written case reports of individuals in the unit, and reviewed Chapter Seven. I am only sorry there was not space to include all of the cases.

Larry Kelly helped guide me through the police world, reviewed Chapters Six and Eight, and found the financial resources that enabled this book to be published. Gratitude is a weak term for all of that.

Erin Zolotukhin-Ridgway from the Central St. Paul Public Library e-mailed me every *St. Paul Pioneer Press* story about Ron Ryan, Tim Jones, and Laser. Thanks to Sue Reiter, Executive Assistant to the Director of the Minnesota Police and Peace Officers Association, for keeping me hydrated while I reviewed over 30 years of the *Minnesota Police Journal*.

I would also like to thank Jason Cook, Deputy Photo Director for the *St. Paul Pioneer Press,* and A.J. Forliti.

As I walked past a dozen or so parked canine police squad cars the other day, the chorus of barking German shepherd dogs made me realize that the dogs deserve the final and certainly not the least word of gratitude. Thanks for every protective bark.

Ruth Gordon
St. Paul, Minnesota
January 31, 2008

Chapter One

The History of Using Dogs in Police Work

Dogs, not humans, came up with the idea of doing police work. The history and evolution of canine police work begins with several famous dogs that apparently did what just came naturally, namely, they protected their owners. After dogs showed humans that they were good crime solvers on their own, humans started thinking that maybe dogs could do even more if they had some special training. How right they were!

The first dog known to solve a crime on his own was never identified by name, but he is famous nonetheless. Sometime between 300–272 BCE during the reign of King Pyrrhus of Epirus, a slave was killed on a lonely road for an unknown reason. The only witness to the murder was the slave's dog, who remained beside his master's body. Several days later, King Pyrrhus, riding in his chariot through the countryside accompanied by his servants and soldiers, came upon the scene. The King, struck by what he saw, stopped, ordered that the man be buried, and commanded that the dog be brought to him. Subsequently, the dog lived with the King and was treated very well. Several weeks later, the King was inspecting his troops with the dog at his side. Suddenly, the dog lunged at two of the soldiers. His attack was relentless and vicious. The two men being attacked recognized the dog and quickly confessed that they had killed the slave. The dog had identified the men who had murdered his master.

The French essayist, Michel de Montaigne, tells the story of another crime-solving dog. His name was Cupparas. He lived in Athens and was assigned to guard the contents of an opulently furnished temple at night. One night Cupparas spotted a thief carrying away some valuable items from the temple. Cupparas barked loudly as the thief started to run. However, no one heard his warnings, so Cupparas followed the thief, not just for awhile but for days and weeks. Cupparas was careful to stay aloof from the thief but he was never far away.

When the dog became hungry, he refused to accept food from the thief, but he fawned over strangers, wagging his tail and accepting their food. Whenever the thief rested from his journeys, the dog also rested nearby. News of this strangely acting dog reached the temple-keepers. They asked witnesses for a detailed description of the dog. Their depiction matched their missing guard dog perfectly. Weeks later the temple representatives found the man in the city of Cromyon by locating their dog who was still watching the man's every move. The thief was arrested and upon returning to Athens, he was punished. Having caught the thief, Cupparas lived out his days receiving special rations from the city of Athens and the temple priests.

Hercules, a large mastiff known as the Dog of Montargis, belonged to a favorite knight of King Charles V of France. However, that knight, Chevalier Aubry de Montdidier, had a jealous enemy, Sieur de Macaire, in the King's court. Macaire carefully arranged a hunting trip with Aubry, who was always accompanied by Hercules. While hunting deep in the woods, Macaire quietly fell behind Aubry. Taking care that no one was around, Macaire charged Aubry from behind with a spear, killing him instantly. Macaire buried Aubry but Hercules stayed behind at the grave site. After a few days, the dog became hungry and went to the castle for food. Whenever Hercules saw Macaire, he growled and snarled. The other knights were baffled by such menacing behavior of the "gentle giant," as Hercules was known. The knights were also very concerned about the prolonged absence of Aubry. When the dog disappeared once more for several days and returned, he growled again when he saw Macaire. Finally, the perplexed knights became suspicious and decided to follow Hercules when he left the castle. Hercules led them straight to Aubry's grave. The dog had, of course, already identified Aubry's killer. Macaire was quickly put to death by order of the King.

A similar incident occurred in England. A dog started coming to a country squire's house looking for food. After eating, the dog would then swim across the water to an island in the Thames. After noting this behavior several times, the squire became so curious about the dog that he got in his boat one day and followed the animal. He found that the dog was tending a body of a brutally beaten man. The squire arranged for the man's burial and brought the dog to live at his home. On a visit to London, the squire, accompanied by the dog, rented a boat for an excursion. On their return to the dock, the dog suddenly hurled himself at a man standing nearby. The squire was puzzled but did not call the dog off. Very soon the terrified man, recognizing the dog, admitted to the murder of the dog's master.

In Greek mythology dogs were famed as hunters, guardians, and loyal defenders. Orion's hunting dog Sirius accompanied his master to eternity in the heavens where they exist today as constellations. When Ulysses finally returned home after being absent for twenty years, his aged dog, Argus, recognized his master despite his ragged clothing. Argus then died happy with the knowledge that his master had returned.

These qualities of endurance, agility, and loyalty have been known in mythology, history, literature, and art. Today, dogs hold a prominent place in our homes as pets. Programs train dogs to help the blind and the disabled and to assist hunters. They are now also valuable colleagues in police work. However, it took humans a long time to realize to what extent a dog's ability to do police work could be developed.

Police work, as we have come to know it, was invented in the early 19th century, and by the middle of the 19th century, there was a professional police force in most cities in the United States. Before 1899, dogs were used mainly to guard property. Then in 1899 the Belgian city of Ghent started the first program in the world to train dogs for law enforcement work. By Christmas of that year, there were 37 dogs on duty every night with their handlers between 10 p.m. and 6 a.m. The commissioner deemed the program both successful and economical. The dogs were on leash at all times, but because the dogs had different handlers almost every night, the dogs apparently led the handlers on their rounds.

The Ghent program attracted worldwide attention and served as a model for almost all future programs. Programs sprang up in other Belgian cities. German police officers visited to learn their training techniques. Within three years, there were 150 German communities with auxiliary police dogs and by 1910, 600 German towns had official programs. Austria, Hungary, Italy, Norway, England, and the United States all started programs in the early 1900s.

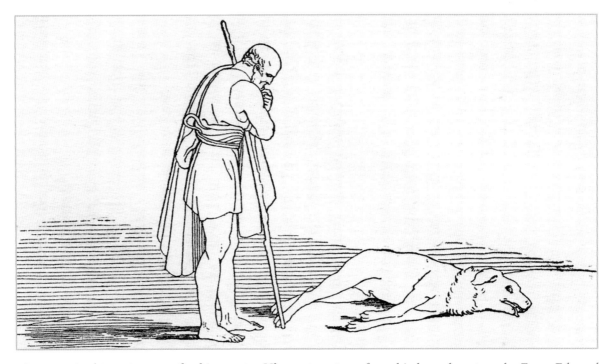

Argus waited twenty years for his master Ulysses to return from his legendary travels. From Edward Brooks, The Story of the Odyssey. *Reprint of 1891 edition (1927), 265.*

Sadly, the pioneering Ghent program was terminated in 1938 in spite of its many successes. Training had encouraged the Ghent dogs to attack anyone not wearing a police uniform. The dogs lacked regular handlers so there were no consistent expectations or discipline of the dogs. Undoubtedly, there were other unpublished reasons for its termination. However, there was never any doubt that the Ghent program had had a profound effect on canine law enforcement programs throughout the world during its 39 years of operation.

During this same period, the Germans improved the training of dogs for police work. After trying several breeds for the work, it was the Germans who identified the German shepherd dog as best suited for the job. Doberman pinschers also worked well. However, the Doberman has a tendency to be unpredictable on occasion, not a desirable quality for police work.

It was the British police who formalized large-scale training and use of police canine units. It came about gradually. They first used Airedales to deal with rowdy sailors and to protect goods on the docks. In other parts of the country, it was common practice for a policeman to bring his own dog on duty to keep him company. It was observed that just the presence of a dog seemed to reduce crime. In 1946, six trained Labrador retrievers were taken into service by the London Metropolitan Police District. In 1951, the Lancashire Constabulary, the second largest in the United Kingdom, began a program in earnest. They had successfully used bloodhounds for tracking, but soon found that bloodhounds have too pleasant a disposition for other kinds of police work. Finally, the British started using Doberman pinschers and German shepherds. By 1987 the United Kingdom had 1,954 dogs serving in canine police units throughout the country.

One of the most famous handler/dog teams in London was that of Constable Arthur Holman and his German shepherd, Rex III. They worked for Scotland Yard, London's Metropolitan Police Force, in the 1950s. The two worked together on hundreds of cases. The dog received many honors: St. Francis religious medals, money, letters from both children and adults, and he had a special audience with the King and Queen. In his book, *My Dog Rex*, Holman expressed what many handlers feel when a dog must stop working. Holman identified the deep bond of love and interdependence between handler and dog. When Holman had to have Rex put down because of throat cancer, he said, "As regards Rex, ours was no ordinary 'master and pet' relationship… Police Dog Rex III was an essential part of my life and being, and still dominates my thoughts and memories. When he died something vital went from me."

At about the same time in the 1950s, another famous canine detective named Dox started solving crimes in Rome. He appears in almost all historical reports. A policeman by the name of Giovanni Maimone in Turin, Italy, once happened to walk by a pet store. He glanced in the window and saw a plump little German shepherd puppy. He had thought about buying a German shepherd, and when this little puppy looked up at him the way all puppies do when they have selected their owner, Giovanni couldn't resist. He bought the dog.

Giovanni decided to name the dog Dox. Then, for fun, he taught him to find things. He would have Dox smell a handkerchief and then hide it in the next room. The dog quickly learned to follow and locate a scent. It was all a game until one day a jewelry store was robbed. The thief had left behind a dirty glove. Giovanni thought this was a good time to test Dox on the job. While the other police officers scoffed at the idea of using a dog, they watched Dox sniff the glove thoroughly. Dox then went out the door and slowly sniffed his way to a busy highway where gasoline fumes and the scents of grass and rubber tires competed with the smell of the glove. Dox suddenly left the highway, turned down a side road and sat down on the front porch of a little house. The police knocked at the door. A woman came outside. She said that her husband was in jail and that no one else was in the house. The police checked her story and learned that her husband had been released from jail several days before the robbery and that he had stopped at his home for a few minutes before running away. Several days later, he was found in the next town. Dox had cracked his first case!

Dox grew to weigh 140 pounds and became known as "Il Gigante," or the giant. Giovanni and Dox had a special birthday ritual. Dox was allowed to visit all his favorite restaurants and eat where and what he wanted. On his thirteenth birthday, Giovanni let Dox sniff in all his favorite restaurants, but it was getting out of hand. "Choose one! I'm hungry," shouted Giovanni. At that very moment, Dox stiffened at the door of a restaurant. As they entered, Dox went straight to a table where a man sat eating spaghetti. Giovanni immediately recognized the man as a criminal who had escaped from the police six years earlier. Dox had been on the case back then and had remembered the man's scent for six years!

Police reports noted that Dox helped catch more than 400 criminals during his career. He received twenty-seven silver and four gold medals for many competitions and distinguished service awards. When Dox was suddenly fired from the force, he had seven bullet wounds and had lost part of an ear. No reason was ever given for his dismissal. In spite of his accomplishments, apparent jealousy forced him into retirement. Furious, Giovanni resigned from the force the day after Dox was dismissed. The two of them soon started Casa Dox, which became a prestigious center for training dogs for private citizens.

The first canine program in the United States started in New York City in 1907. It was terminated in 1951. The dogs had had multiple handlers, worked off-leash, and there had been many mistakes on the job. After World War II, over 100 towns and cities started canine units only to drop them after a few years.

Even when police administrators felt that canines were effective in law enforcement, programs often failed because of one or more of the following reasons:

★ Public perception of dogs as fanged symbols of oppression
★ Inadequate funding because of a lack of commitment to the idea
★ Lack of acceptance by the public and/or by police departments
★ Difficulty in procuring suitable animals when necessary characteristics were not yet well-defined
★ Shortage of competent trainers
★ Need for better training and continued in-service training
★ Some error that caused a fatal accident to an innocent person

The Baltimore, Maryland, police force launched the first major U. S. program in 1957. They had recruited 15 dogs the year before and hired a former military dog trainer. After demonstrating many successes, the K-9 corps was formally incorporated into the police department. Their success prompted other cities to emulate their methods and by 1970 more than 80 police departments used dogs in their patrol force. St. Paul, Minnesota, initiated the second program in the United States in 1958, but it lasted only three years. In 1972, St. Paul's canine program was reestablished and went on to become one of the most outstanding in the country.

Canine units shared information with one another. The value of understanding dog psychology, not just human psychology, was shared by Sergeant William Horton of the New York State Police. He demonstrated how this important knowledge could be used in practice. He knew that his two bloodhounds were very jealous of each other in a work situation. Sergeant Horton used that jealousy to track a dangerous criminal accused of killing a state trooper. The man had fled into a densely forested area that was surrounded by police. Horton tied one of his dogs to the back of his car and then went into the woods with his other dog straining on the leash. The dog tied to the car was beside himself. He burst into incredible moans of frustration and jealousy. The dog's baying and frustrating howls could be heard throughout the area. The killer froze. He was from the south and the thought of bloodhounds chasing him was terrifying. He started a desperate run out of the woods and found himself right in front of the pointed guns of friends of the slain trooper. Once the killer was captured, Horton and his leashed dog came out of the thicket, barely a few feet away from his dog tied to the car.

The use of dogs in Canada is somewhat different from other countries because of the vast expanses of uninhabited land. In 1990, only Ontario and Quebec used dogs in law enforcement. The main use of dogs is by the Royal Canadian Mounted Police (RCMP) in search and rescue operations. Dogs and their handlers are stationed at various RCMP centers across the country. The teams are in constant readiness to respond to requests to locate missing persons who may be lost in an avalanche or blizzard, to track criminals, to engage in bomb and narcotic detection, to guard prisoners, and to find evidence from a crime scene. Sled dogs may be used for transportation in remote areas.

Because so much of the work of dogs in Canada relates to search and rescue, a dog's morale becomes extremely important. Search and Rescue (S&R) dogs learn that the reward of "the game" is to find someone alive. If they do not find anyone, they become depressed and cannot work well. This was a special problem for the S&R dogs working at New York's World Trade Center on September 11, 2001. Handlers of course also become depressed and frustrated when they are not successful in finding survivors and dogs sense their handlers' depression. To alleviate the situation, handlers often needed to set up "pretend" or practice search situations where the dog can find someone alive and feel successful. Afterward they were able to return to their work.

Without a doubt the greatest number of S&R dogs sent to aid in the aftermath of a disaster on American soil were those deployed to New York and Washington, D.C., after 9/11. In her book, *Dog Heroes of September 11th*, Nona Kilgore Bauer estimated that 250 to 300 K-9 teams went to those sites. These dogs, sent from units throughout the country, were trained as cadaver or live find dogs. Breeds used included Labrador retrievers, Belgian Malinois, German shepherds, border collies, golden retrievers, and Doberman pinschers. DOGNY was the American Kennel Club's public art salute to the work of these S&R canine heroes.

The idea of using dogs in police work is now accepted worldwide. There are national standards and guidelines for policies and procedures for administering such a unit in police departments in the United States. In 1971, two canine associations combined to form the U.S. Police Canine Association, Inc. Its annual seminar presents new ideas and training techniques. It is a repository of information for agencies that are considering starting a department. The association also promotes working standards and it certifies dog teams according to strict professional criteria. Every year this organization sponsors the National Police Canine Trials. This brings the best U.S. and foreign canine teams to be judged by nationally certified judges. Great strides have been made in elevating and standardizing training through this association.

Selection of dogs is crucial to the success of any program. Therefore, evaluation of candidate dogs is a necessary beginning. A dog must have intelligence, agility, a good olfactory sense, a willingness to learn, stamina, and emotional stability, combined with a suitable amount of aggressiveness, which can be transformed into courage. Experience indicates that a good age for training is between 10 and 24 months. Even with good

Robert Braun's bronze statue of a German shepherd was selected as the model for over 100 decorated DOGNY sculptures exhibited in New York City in 2002. The sculptures honored heroic dogs and people who worked in search and rescue efforts after September 11, 2001. Courtesy of the American Kennel Club.

screening tools, almost one-third of the dogs initially selected do not end up becoming police dogs. The German shepherd is presently the breed of choice. Unfortunately, since 9/11, dogs are in great demand and in short supply. Many departments prefer to purchase dogs from European kennels, but these dogs are quite expensive.

A good program starts with a well-trained dog. Training is arduous work for both the dog and the handler. It usually lasts about 12 weeks. Dogs learn obedience, tracking, article retrieval, how to search an area, agility, criminal apprehension on command, and handler protection. Some dogs are also cross-trained in bomb and/or narcotics detection. Training of trainers is an essential national goal of the U.S. Police Canine Association.

Handlers must also be screened. Several state police departments have published criteria for handler selection. Some of the Virginia State Police criteria for handler selection include the following:

★ It must be a voluntary decision to work with dogs
★ An applicant must be very fond of dogs
★ The officer's family must be willing to enjoy the dog at home
★ An applicant's living environment must be accepting of dogs
★ Prefer men and women under the age of forty
★ Handlers need to love the outdoors
★ Willing to spend the extra time it requires to care for and practice with the dog to maintain its skills

As noted, the use of dogs in police work began over 2,000 years ago in a remote part of Europe when King Pyrrhus found a dog guarding its master's grave. Today, most people will agree that dogs can be advantageous to a police department and that they are here to stay. Dogs can have a psychological effect in crowd control and in deterring criminal activity. Dogs help track lost children and elderly persons who have lost their way. They protect police officers and they aid police in detecting and capturing suspects in alleys, backyards, and wooded areas, especially at night. Their searches not only locate people but also stolen property and traces of evidence. Canines and their partners also educate their communities through demonstrations of what the dogs can do. Their friendly presence in parks, beaches, local fairs, and shopping malls creates an image of safety. Some police executives report that in crowd control and search situations an officer with a trained dog can be as effective as up to ten officers without trained dogs. That may or may not be an overstatement but it is a fact that canine police units have significant economic benefits.

Chapter Two

The First Use of Police Dogs in St. Paul

One month after St. Paul was incorporated as a city in 1854, the city council elected William R. Miller to the new position of City Marshal. He apparently worked alone until 1858 when the City Marshal post was eliminated and replaced by an appointed Chief of Police. As Chief of Police, Miller appointed four assistants to help him with the work for a city then numbering 4,000 residents. People who were arrested on suspicion of murder, theft, and public drunkenness had to be incarcerated at Fort Snelling. St. Paul clearly needed a jail. The first structure built for that purpose was erected in 1857 on the site of the present Landmark Center.

Murder, robbery, prostitution, and gambling increased as immigrants flocked to Minnesota. The police force increased to twelve and was supported by 40 unpaid men known as the "Vigilance Committee." When the Civil War began in 1861, so many St. Paul police officers enlisted in the army that the police force was disbanded and two hundred volunteers were recruited to take its place. They were referred to as the "Home Guard." In 1863, a new police force was organized with ten men. After the Civil War, poverty, ethnic antagonisms, vice, gambling, drunkenness, seven brothels, and 242 saloons kept the police busy in St. Paul.

Communication between early police officers was quite creative. They signaled to one another by using their night sticks and whistles (one rap or whistle if help was needed and three raps or whistles for real emergencies).

In the 1930s, police had only one-way (receiving) radios. Police headquarters personnel were allowed to interrupt KSTP commercial radio programming in order to communicate to a police officer when an incident needed attention. However, there was always the question of whether the officer actually received the message. In addition, the general public and the suspects could also tune in and hear the messages. Stanley Hubbard of Hubbard Broadcasting (KSTP) saw the problem and built a separate

station only for police use. Finally, in 1939, two-way radios became available, so it was assured that a sent message would be received. Today, there is a mobile data terminal (M.D.T.) in every squad car so an officer can gain quick access to motor vehicle registries and crime information from local, state, and national sources.

In the early days, police walked, rode a bicycle, or sometimes rode horseback. It was not easy to transport law-breakers. Officers had to make do with whatever was handy, which sometimes meant using a wheelbarrow. In 1856, a local grocer donated his horse-drawn wagon for night police work (he used it for his work during the day). Soon there were horse-drawn wagons, known as Black Marias or paddy wagons (a derogatory nickname referring to Irish immigrants) in service until 1934. In 1909, two motorcycles became available. In St. Paul, the first automobile was used by the police in 1912. Several of the department's vehicles, including the paddy wagons, are in view in the new Western District Station at 389 North Hamline Avenue.

Women, known as police inspectors, were employed in the late 19th century, but they were mainly used as jail matrons until 1913 when "policewoman" became a legitimate Civil Service position. However, the women wore plain clothes and usually worked with juveniles. The first uniformed female patrol officer, Deborah Montgomery, was hired in St. Paul in 1975, even though the International Policewomen's Association (now the Association of Women Police)

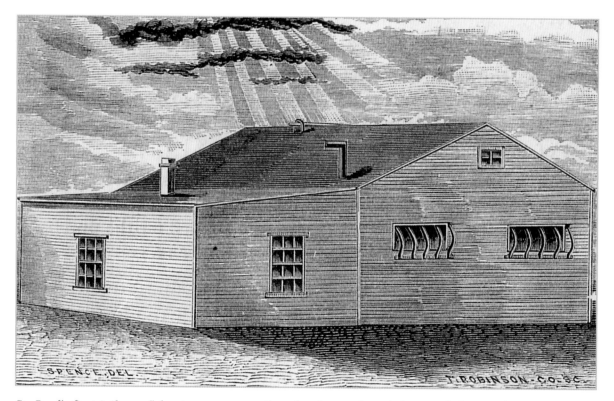

St. Paul's first jail was "about as secure as if made of paste-board. It served the city from 1851-1857."
J. Fletcher Williams, A History of the City of St. Paul *(1876), 281.*

The horse-drawn workhouse van was used until 1934. It is now displayed in the Western District Police Station. Courtesy of the author.

Founders of the St. Paul Police Canine Unit and their dogs stand on the steps of the Minnesota State Capitol. They are (left to right) Bill Swiger and Champ, Larry McDonald and Pal, Ed Buehlman and Baron. Courtesy of Larry McDonald.

was begun in 1915, five years before the U.S. Constitution was amended to grant women the right to vote in 1920. It was not until the passage of the Woman's Suffrage Amendment that St. Paul women were able to become sworn officers because a 1912 legal opinion said one had to be a legal voter to have the authority to make arrests. Patrol officer badges read "patrolman" until 1985 when they were changed to read "patrol officer." Lynn Sorenson became the first female canine officer with her dog, Kato, in 1989.

The idea of adding dogs to the police force actually started in 1955 when 24-year-old Laurence (Larry) Francis McDonald joined the St. Paul police force. He was appointed patrolman in July of that year in the Tactical Division. Larry McDonald had a high school diploma, and upon employment, received one month of what is called "on-the-job training" today. The subjects of his training included first aid, local ordinances, how to fill out accident reports, use of firearms, and city geography. At that time, there were no schools or books to educate new recruits except for a police manual from the Los Angeles Police Department. After this brief introduction to police work, a new recruit then worked with another officer for a month or two. However, McDonald says that he and other officers received excellent continuing education opportunities throughout their careers. During his 40-year career, he took so many courses from colleges and universities that he ended up teaching many courses himself and retired as a Commander in 1995.

McDonald made many innovative suggestions to the department throughout his career, but one of his first ideas related to his frustration in trying to find culprits hidden away in buildings, especially at night. When police were searching on foot, they only had their own ears and eyes and a flashlight with undependable batteries. One night McDonald and Ed Buehlman were standing next to a fence watching for a runaway. McDonald said, "You know, Ed, we can't possibly jump over that fence, but if we had a dog, the dog could jump the fence." They talked then about how they knew that they and others were missing many opportunities to find lawbreakers.

Larry McDonald remembered when he and his brothers used to visit their four bachelor uncles who lived on a farm. The young boys spent a lot of time with their uncles' dogs: red bones (a southern breed of hunter), black and tan coonhounds, and walker hounds (also known as nose dogs). With those dogs, he and his brothers were able to track sheep, foxes, raccoons, squirrels, and other animals. They could even track each other when one brother hid somewhere.

McDonald kept thinking about the possibility of a dog helping police to track people on the run. In fact, he thought a lot about this idea. Then one day he heard that the city of Baltimore, Maryland, was looking for dogs to do police work. It just so happened that McDonald was getting married. The date was June 7, 1958, and it seemed like a perfect arrangement if he and his bride spent their honeymoon at Niagara Falls and then stopped off in Baltimore to check out the canine program before coming home.

The people who had started the new Baltimore program had initially decided not to emulate the British model. British police carried no weapons and used Labrador retrievers to knock a person down by grabbing a person's clothing. British police dogs protected their handlers and helped in crowd control. The Americans, on the other hand, dealt with criminals who were more likely to use knives and guns when confronted by police. Because of this difference, the Baltimore police had decided to use dogs that would bite. They first researched the training of military dogs, particularly sentry dogs. Therefore, they started by using a military dog trainer. As McDonald talked with the Baltimore group, he discovered that they knew an expert dog trainer named Al Johnson who lived in West St. Paul. Finding such a resource right at home was a remarkable turn of events.

After the McDonalds returned home, Larry called Al Johnson, who was also intrigued by the idea of training dogs for police work. Sergeant John Mercado, the head of the Tactical Unit, also thought the idea of using police dogs had merit. When Mercado went to Chief of Police Bill Proetz about the idea, the Chief suggested that they take Al Johnson to lunch to talk it over. At the end of lunch, they all agreed it was worth a try. Al Johnson, however, made one sobering statement, "You know that your officers will need more training than the dogs." That made McDonald a bit anxious just as similar words have made every pet owner apprehensive when taking a dog for obedience training for the first time.

Because there were no public funds for such a "frivolous" idea, Al Johnson sought breeders who were willing to donate three good German shepherds for the project. In addition to Larry McDonald, officers Ed Buehlman and Bill Swiger volunteered to train with the dogs. McDonald and Buehlman had worked the 6 p.m. to 2 a.m. shift together on the east side of St. Paul. One would walk Payne Avenue. The other would walk Arcade Avenue. Then together, they walked the Rondo and St. Anthony bars. The Turtle Club could always be counted on for lively activities. Swiger, a man known for remembering every joke he ever heard, was a friend of both men, so he became the third handler.

Johnson found three purebred German shepherds. Larry's dog was Pal, Ed's dog was Baron, and Bill's dog was Champ. It was 1958. These six canines and humans pioneered the first use of dogs in the St. Paul Police Department.

Al Johnson and his associate, Bob Gates, another nationally recognized dog trainer, volunteered their time. The three dogs moved in with the officers' families. Besides their training with Johnson and Gates, the men worked with their dogs after they came home from work. The cost of the dogs' food, veterinary bills, and licenses were absorbed by the officers as well as the cost of using their own automobiles. In addition, after training or working in mud and rain, their clothing smelled "like a dog," which McDonald said made for many very expensive dry cleaning bills.

Larry McDonald and his dog Pal confront another patrolman, Ed Kaase, during attack practice. Kaase wears a protective bite suit. Courtesy of Ed Buehlman.

Training started with obedience, which was strongly emphasized. A dog that was told to attack must do so, but do so only on command. After mastering obedience came tracking-in-building searches, and then the dogs learned more aggressive behaviors. As the partners became more and more "professional," they began to work in the field. At first there were more skeptics than supporters in the department, but both time and results would be the judge.

At this time, the city started to have an epidemic of damaging school break-ins. Police could not be everywhere and there were no alarms in the schools. McDonald decided that the dogs would be perfect for this kind of problem. The schools would be a good place for training. He obtained the keys to every school and he received permission to use the schools for that purpose. McDonald made sure that the dog teams rotated to different schools each night. Once the word was out, fear of the dogs and the unpredictability of their whereabouts radically reduced the number of school break-ins.

Public education was (and still is) vitally important. The three handlers put on demonstrations of their dogs' obedience, had them do some tricks and demonstrate their ability to follow a scent. They went to schools, PTA meetings, Boy Scout outings, and Elk, Lion, Kiwanis, and Rotary club meetings. They did not wear their gun belts on these occasions because they thought that a dog *and* a gun might be too intimidating. On one occasion,

Ed Buehlman and Baron, Larry McDonald and Pal, Bill Swiger and Champ, 1959. Courtesy of Ed Buehlman.

1270 Barclay
St. Paul 6, Minn.
December 10, 1959

Dear Officer Buhlman,

    Thank you for bringing Baron to Prosperity Heights School on Wednesday. I am sure our whole school enjoyed it.

    How is your job and how is Baron? Have you caught any burglars yet? I hope you do not have to work on Christmas. Thank you again.

                    Your friend,
                    Tim Swanberg

Thank-you note written to Ed Buehlman after he and his dog Baron made a school appearance in 1959. Courtesy of Ed Buehlman.

Baron waits while his handler Ed Buehlman receives information. Courtesy of Ed Buehlman.

Ed Buehlman met the man who had donated his dog, Baron, to the program. The donor said, "I would never have given him away if I had known what that dog could learn to do."

With a lot of work, the three pairs laid a solid base for acceptance of using police dogs. In addition, they were successful in their work. An undated newspaper account stated, "In the eight months the K9 Corps has been in service, they have been used successfully in the apprehension of hold-up men, burglars, car thieves, window peepers, and crowd control."

The public especially liked to read about the dogs in specific situations that demonstrated the dogs' special abilities. In 1959 the Albrecht Fur Company, located at 21 West 5th Street, was having a frequent problem with a very clever and elusive burglar. The building had been searched more than once by regular officers who suspected that the man was in the building whenever the electric alarm had sounded. However, they could not find him. Finally, they reluctantly called in a dog team. Even in doing so, they expressed doubt that the team could do any better than they had. Bill Swiger and his dog Champ entered the building and soon found the burglar concealed behind some plywood paneling. Champ not only found his man but gave this master burglar a good bite, on command, of course. For this, Champ won the National Lassie Award, given annually by the popular television program to a dog for outstanding work. This was the first award ever won by a St. Paul canine, surely a glimpse into the group's future performance.

Some amusing episodes occurred in those early days. One morning, McDonald and Pal were sent to St. Joseph's Academy, a Catholic girls' school, because an escapee from a woman's prison was hiding inside. The young woman had outrun everyone, including the police. Finally, the police were able to chase her out into the street where Larry McDonald and Pal were waiting for her. McDonald shouted, "Stop!" but she kept on running so Pal was released from his leash. Pal not only stopped her, but he also bit her. When the girl was treated for her dog bite, the doctors discovered she had syphilis. The doctors told McDonald to put Pal into quarantine immediately! Fortunately, someone consulted the University of Minnesota Veterinary Clinic, who assured everyone that a dog cannot get syphilis from a person nor could the dog transmit syphilis to a human being. Pal went back to work the next day.

McDonald says, "Believe the dog." One night he and Pal were tracking a window peeper in Highland Park. They could not find the man anywhere on the ground. However, Pal kept looking up at the roof. Finally, McDonald also looked up. Pal had seen the young man, who had climbed up the copper drain pipe to the roof.

Looking beyond his own line of sight saved McDonald more than once. One winter night two squad cars were called to Selby Avenue. Larry McDonald was in one of them.

He looked up at a second floor apartment and saw a man with a raised rifle pointed out the window right at them. McDonald yelled to the other officer, "Get out of here!" They sped off as best they could, which was tricky because the street was icy. When they returned to the apartment to make an arrest, they found all kinds of illegal ammunition. Pal had taught him well.

Another night McDonald and Buehlman came upon two detectives struggling in the middle of a crowd of drunken, swearing, rock-throwing citizens. It was particularly violent, so Pal was released from his leash. After Pal took a large chunk out of one woman's buttock, things calmed down. The woman, who had to be hospitalized, never sued because it was clear that she had been assaulting a police detective. Convalescing at home was certainly better than in prison.

During the 1920s and 1930s, under what became famous as the O'Connor policy (Chief of Police William O'Connor initiated it), criminals would not be arrested in St. Paul for crimes committed elsewhere, as long as they behaved themselves in the Saintly City. Paul Maccabee explains this history in his book *John Dillinger Slept Here* (1995). The policy ended when the Barker-Karpis gang kidnapped local businessmen William Hamm and Edward Bremer in 1933–34. By that time respect for the St. Paul police department was at an all-time low. Some officials thought that changing the color of the uniform to green might give the police a new image. In 1931, green uniforms were initiated. Unfortunately, most police officers thought the new uniforms made them look like Texaco Company gas station attendants. There were no patches on the shirts, and they were just plain "ugly" according to all reports. One day Buehlman had to give a demonstration to a group with his dog. He was so embarrassed by his uniform that he asked a lieutenant to give him some patches to wear. The lieutenant gave him some patches to wear for the day but asked that Buehlman return them after his program. Finally, in 1964 the uniforms were changed back to blue; the fabric was selected by two student interns studying textiles at the College of St. Catherine.

The canine program continued to be a success, but in 1961 a new Chief of Police was appointed. Chief Proetz left his position and was succeeded by Chief Lester McAuliffe. According to several sources, Proetz and McAuliffe did not get along well and disagreed about many things, one of which was the use of dogs in the department. As a result, McAuliffe assigned the three Canine Unit founders to other duties and St. Paul had no canine unit for the next eleven years.

Ending the program in St. Paul was very hard on the dogs as well as the men. The dogs became anxious and depressed when they were told to stay home while their handlers put on their uniforms and went off to work. The dogs made wonderful family pets but they still had a lot of energy and a desire for work. Larry McDonald was an avid walker, so he and Pal would go for one- and two-mile walks after he came off duty in the early morning hours. Unexpectedly, Pal got one more chance to work one night. When Larry and Pal returned home, they found three men hiding on McDonald's porch! They had escaped from the police after robbing a nearby bar. Not expecting anyone at that hour and not knowing whose porch it was, the three were routed out when Pal and McDonald got busy. They drove the culprits into a quarry and into the hands of the police. Although unofficial, that was the last St. Paul Police K-9 job done between 1961 and 1972, when the program began again.

Larry McDonald eventually returned to the Canine Unit twice before retiring as a Commander in 1995. Edward Buehlman never returned to the Canine Unit and retired in 1977. McDonald and Buehlman continue to be close friends in retirement and both contributed to the writing of this book. William Swiger never returned to the Canine Unit and retired in 1976. Swiger died of cancer on December 20, 1993.

Chapter Three

Police Dogs Return to St. Paul

During the eleven years (1961–72) when the St. Paul Police Department had no dogs, many shocking events jolted the country. Opposition to the Vietnam War escalated into more and more contentious public demonstrations. Ultimately, some 250,000 people marched on Washington, D.C., in 1969. In Selma and Birmingham, Alabama, dogs were allowed to be vicious in quelling civil rights demonstrators in 1963. Martin Luther King, Jr., was assassinated on April 4, 1968, and two months later, Robert Kennedy was shot in a Los Angeles hotel. The anti-war demonstrations at Kent State University resulted in the Ohio National Guard killing four students in 1970. At the Democratic Convention held in Chicago in 1968, large and violent racial and anti-war demonstrations erupted. Mayor Daly ordered in the National Guard to assist the police in crowd control. Dogs were used again in a way that would never be condoned today. The unprecedented violence in Chicago resulted in many serious injuries on both sides. A public uproar about the way the crowd was handled led to hearings, reviews, and reports for many years to come. Rock concerts with excessive drug use added to the turmoil. These explosive events of the '60s damaged the reputation of police departments across the country. Every corner of the United States was affected and St. Paul was no exception.

In St. Paul two officers, James Sackett and Glen Kothe, were ambushed when they responded to a fake call for medical help on May 22, 1970. Sackett was killed and his killers, while they had been long suspected, were not convicted of the murder until thirty-six years later, in 2006. It was thought that the motive for killing a cop at that time was to gain the attention of national Black Panther leaders in hopes of getting a Black Panther chapter started in St. Paul. In 1970, witnesses refused to give any information about the shooting. Thirty-six years later, the same witnesses finally did testify, adding that

James Cocchiarella, head trainer, instructs patrolman Larry Nevin and his dog Jubal on how to attack a suspect. Nevin wears a protective bite sleeve. Courtesy of Larry Nevin.

given the rigid code of silence back in 1970, it would have been suicide for anyone to have come forward with the truth.

The second chapter in the use of police dogs in St. Paul occurred in 1972 when racial tensions were still very much alive. There was a growing need for additional police manpower and a genuine desire for more innovative methods of law enforcement. It was thought that the proper use of dogs could help achieve both goals. One St. Paul police officer, James Cocchiarella, bred German shepherds and taught obedience training in the community. He owned Jubal, a purebred German shepherd that he had trained to do some tracking. Convinced that dogs could enhance the capability of the police, Cocchiarella was able to convince Deputy Chief William McCutcheon and Chief Richard Rowan to approve the establishment of two dog teams to be trained and available for work with other St. Paul officers. Cocchiarella would be one of the two handlers.

Chief Rowan did not know who the second handler might be. However, by chance, while Officer Glen Kothe was attending an in-service training program, someone mentioned the need for a helicopter. Kothe's response was, "Hell, a helicopter can't get in a building like a dog could." His life-long interest in dogs was known and he became the second handler. Kothe served with the Canine Unit for the next 10 years and was promoted to Sergeant a year after he left the unit.

By the 1970s Minneapolis had a very good training center for canine police handlers. Lieutenant Michael Fisher had been trained as a handler and as a trainer at the Washington, D.C., Police Department. Fisher became the Head Trainer at the Minneapolis center, which had received a federal grant to train handler teams for Minneapolis and for other communities.

James Cocchiarella brought his own German shepherd, Jubal, and Glen Kothe brought a donated dog named Reggie to the Minneapolis Handler Training School. Reggie was a purebred German shepherd that had been owned by a family with three children. The little boy in the family had developed allergies to the dog, so reluctantly the family had to give up Reggie. However, the little boy insisted that the dog become a police dog. The youngster was thrilled that Glen Kothe, a police officer, was going to take his dog to school to learn how to be a police dog. In 1972, after completing handler training, the two officers and their canine partners started work. They were assigned to be on call with the patrol division.

When canine officers are asked to tell about some of their experiences, they inevitably wonder, "Where to begin?" Kothe had two stories, one to illustrate the speed of his dog and the other to illustrate the dog's incredibly innate sense of danger.

One winter night Kothe and Reggie were called to the Hart Ski Company. They were the first to arrive. They found footprints in the snow leading to an entrance that had been broken open. When they entered the building, Kothe could hear several people running up a stairway. He released Reggie, who streaked up the stairs passing what turned out to be five suspects. Reggie suddenly stopped and turned around to face the men as they approached up the stairs. When the men turned around to run the other way, there stood Kothe at the bottom of the stairs with gun drawn. When the back-up officers arrived, the five men were already handcuffed and lying on the floor face down. Kothe asked the leader where they had put the instrument they used to enter the building. When there was no response, he said, "Reggie, you go ask him." Reggie had been taught to "smile" on command by raising his lips and showing his teeth, so he leaned over to the spokesman's face and smiled. Kothe got his answer.

Another night Kothe was on foot with Reggie watching him from the car. Kothe had left a car window open so Reggie could get out if he needed to call him for help. When Kothe stopped two men on the street for a routine check of identification, Reggie leapt out of the car window without being called and growled menacingly at one of the men. Kothe discovered that the man Reggie had identified was carrying a gun hidden in his clothing. At Reggie's urging, the man turned the gun over to Kothe. What made Reggie come to Kothe's aid without being called? No one knows. But Kothe says that Reggie frequently seemed to sense danger before Kothe was aware of it. If Reggie tensed up when they were together, Kothe knew he was being alerted to danger. This is called "reading your dog" and it is a critical element of training. Dogs signal a handler in individual ways by stopping, growling, raising the hackles, or just tensing up.

Because of Kothe's and Cocchiarella's successes with their dogs, it was decided that three more teams would be trained if it was not going to cost anything. Cocchiarella went to Washington, D.C., to learn to become a trainer. He studied with a Mr. Cahill from London. Mr. Cahill was quite a proper man so no one ever learned his first name. When Cocchiarella returned home, he became the assistant trainer to Michael Fisher in Minneapolis.

Minneapolis donated three dogs for the next St. Paul officers who were to be trained as handlers. They were: Lawrence Nevin, whose dog was Duke; Donald Bulver, whose dog was Baron; and Donald Martin, whose dog was Lobo. When the three officers finished their training, they were ready for work and went on the streets on July 14, 1973. That same year Joseph Renteria and his dog Lance moved from Minneapolis to join the St. Paul Unit.

Larry Nevin tells of the day that he and Duke spent searching for a missing toddler. For over an hour, they tracked through an overgrown field. It was hot and humid. Both Duke and Nevin needed water and rest. As they were trudging along, Duke's ears went up suddenly, he barked, and he stopped. Duke had found the child sound asleep in the field. Nevin picked up the child and put her on his shoulders. As they left the field and became visible to the bystanders, the mother came rushing out to meet them. Nevin yelled at the mother to stand back and not to come a step closer. As Nevin put it, "Duke's hackles were standing up and he was ready to defend me from the woman who appeared [to Duke] to be about to assault me. We didn't need any more excitement for that day."

Office Glen Kothe and Reggie on evening patrol, fall of 1972 or early 1973. Courtesy of Glen Kothe.

In 1975, five more teams trained in Minneapolis. They were Thomas Burke, Mark Klinge, James Long, Donald McAdams, and Archie Smith. Donald Slavik and his dog King were trained separately and then joined the others. In late 1975, the canine group was given full unit designation and it had expanded to 12 teams. James Cocchiarella became St. Paul's first Head Trainer in that year.

These men were dedicated to their work and developed a close bond. They worked many extra hours with their dogs and they spent a lot of their own money on dog food, supplies, and even veterinary care, especially in the first years before there was a budget for canine work. They protected each other and they also had fun playing tricks on each other. They were proud of their accomplishments, which often entailed a great deal of courage. They also wanted other officers on the force to see what their dogs could do. However, they shared one fear—they worried that a dog might bite the wrong person at the wrong time. They knew that such an incident could jeopardize the whole program. That is why Nevin became so nervous when the little girl's mother came running toward him. That is why Cocchiarella insisted that they all have ten hours of retraining every month. That is why Smith panicked when his dog, Luger, ran away one Halloween night when neighborhood children were everywhere doing tricks or treats. Fortunately, Luger had simply gone courting and was found in about an hour.

Archie Smith worked in the Canine Unit for ten years and his dog, Luger, became the first narcotics dog. Smith and Cocchiarella spent hours training Luger. On one of Luger's first jobs, Smith and Luger went to a suspicious house where Luger kept hanging around the garbage can. While the family remained on the sofa, Smith wondered if the dog might just be smelling steak bones, but when he opened the garbage can, he found a stash of marijuana. As the team left through the front door, Luger displeased the little boy in the family by grabbing his snow boot and shaking it fiercely. Luger had found another supply of marijuana, which was kept near to the front door where it could be sold quickly.

Oddly, other officers continued to think that a dog was not really valuable for narcotics searches. However, one Sunday, officers of the Drug Enforcement Administration, a federal agency, called Smith on his day off. They had seen Smith and Luger do a narcotics demonstration and asked for their help.

Several officers along with Luger and Smith arrived at a gated mansion in Minneapolis. When the owner happened to drive up, they searched the car and found a small amount of cocaine. The other officers, leaving Smith and Luger outside, went into the mansion, searched the house, and found nothing. They came out and were about to leave but decided to search the garage. This time Smith and Luger joined them. The men found nothing but Luger found a spot where he stubbornly stayed while staring up at the ceiling. It turned out that Luger's nose had identified 2.2 pounds of cocaine above the ceiling in the garage rafters. Smith says, "That episode had a ripple effect of new believers in what a dog could do."

Rex, Glen Kothe's second dog, was also cross-trained in narcotics work. Rex made front page news when he sniffed out five pounds of hashish and five pounds of cocaine at the airport.

With twelve canine teams now working, the need for their own training center in St. Paul became apparent. The St. Paul Water Department donated a large piece of land adjacent to their operation in Maplewood and a small building was then planned. Some of the unit's officers thought the size of the building was going to be too small, so one or two of them moved the stakes out a considerable distance. This story seems believable because of the strong, proud personalities involved and the number of men who told this story.

In order to keep their dogs trained, they had to find places to work them. Without a place of their own, they had to move around to several locations. One of the places they used was the A-2 Team house located at Art's Towing Company at Jackson and Maryland. All of the damaged, towed vehicles made it look like a junkyard. Reportedly, that is where the term "junkyard dogs" came from. Their building was probably completed in 1975, but the original plaque is undated.

In 1982, to keep pace with rising crime rates, violence, and increased drug trafficking, the unit expanded to 21 teams. The dogs became more and more expert at tracking and apprehending fleeing criminals, searching buildings for suspects, protecting officers in dangerous situations, searching for narcotics and explosives, controlling large crowds, searching for lost children and confused elderly persons, and other activities that make use of a dog's keen sense of smell and its speed in helping make arrests.

As the group grew, one or two officers were selected to help train new dog/handler teams. This was in addition to their street duty. After Officer James Long became the Head Trainer in 1980, the unit started to train teams not only for St. Paul, but for other law enforcement departments throughout the Midwest. The St. Paul Police Canine Unit became recognized throughout the United States and Canada for having exceptional personnel, dogs, training facilities, and progressive and innovative training methods.

Four women joined the Canine Unit before 2000. The first was Lynn Sorenson with her dog, Kato, in 1989. She was followed by Catherine Pavlak and her dog, Dillon, in 1994 and Molly Schwartz and her dog, Sable, in 1996. Teri Learmont and her single-purpose narcotics detector dog, Jessie, were members of the unit from 1998 to 2001.

In 1990, many canine units in police departments throughout the country came under the scrutiny of the Department of Labor for possible violations of the Fair

Employment Labor Standards Act in regard to overtime pay. Canine officers worked 40-hour weeks, but they spent additional hours caring for their dogs. They were not being paid for the time it took to clean the kennels, groom, exercise, and maintain their dogs' skills. Some units were required to give their officers back pay for this time and some shortened the work week slightly. St. Paul decided to pay officers ten hours for every nine hours they worked. This issue is contentious wherever it is debated because it can probably never be fully resolved. In some places, the acrimony has actually caused termination of some canine units.

In 1995, a year after the deaths of Ron Ryan and Tim Jones and Jones' dog Laser (discussed in Chapter Six), Chief of Police William Finney made an agreement with the Police Federation that there would be an officer rotation system in and out of the Canine Unit. Other officers apparently wanted to become canine handlers, partly because they wanted to work with dogs and partly because they felt there was more prestige in being a canine handler. This system would give them the chance.

Similar issues are often reported in other police departments across the country. Some canine programs have even been closed because of administrative and morale problems within a police department. Compensatory time or pay for training and tending dogs may cause jealousy as well as the fact that the public is especially attracted to media stories that include dogs. Officers in other units also become annoyed if they perceive the Canine Unit as an elite group. Tensions were not absent in St. Paul.

It is difficult to assess the degree of tension that existed in 1995. However, this problem was not new in St. Paul. Chief William McCutcheon had started a policy of "one dog and then out." In fact, when Glen Kothe's second dog, Rex, was injured, Kothe was transferred out of the unit. Nonetheless, Chief Finney's announced plan created an intense response. Dave Boll and his dog, Rondo, five-time national team champions, were forced to rotate out of the unit. In response to this transfer, James Long, head trainer for fifteen years, then quit the unit, which resulted in the cancellation of the spring handler training class. Three others were given involuntary transfers. They were Brad Jacobsen, Frank Verdeja, and Lynn Sorenson, the first woman canine handler. It was a very difficult time for the unit. Officers who were transferred out of the unit were especially upset about the morale of their dogs. They felt their dogs still had some years of work life remaining and that they were forced to become household pets prematurely.

Today, except for an extraordinary reason, a canine team works together until a dog can no longer be effective. The handler may get a second dog or be transferred to another unit. The decision depends on many factors which are reviewed by an administrative panel. Trainers will almost always get a second dog.

In 1996, the Canine Unit added four Labrador retrievers for narcotics detection. They joined the other seventeen canine teams in the unit. In 1997, the unit offered its first course in narcotics detection for organizations outside of St. Paul. In 2000, it was thought that single-purpose narcotics detector dogs were not needed when there already were cross-trained dogs in the Canine Unit. However, with increasing narcotics problems, Mark Wiegel and his single-purpose narcotics detector dog, Sully, trained for the Force Unit where they were assigned in December 2006. In 2007, one other single-purpose dog and handler team were trained and assigned to the Narcotics Unit.

In 1997, the St. Paul Police's canine training center was renamed. In honor of Timothy Jones and his K-9 partner Laser, the training center was dedicated as the Timothy J. Jones Canine Training Facility.

Entering the new century, the St. Paul Police Canine Unit has become a nationally known group of men and women who have every reason to be proud of their work. To date, they have trained 356 dogs. They have had hundreds of successes in finding lost persons, getting their bad guys, and saving lives. Their many awards for work performed and in national competitions attest to the caliber of the unit. Both recognition and awards are discussed in Chapter Seven.

Chapter Four

Education and Training of the Handlers

From the beginning of St. Paul law enforcement in the mid-1800s until 1950, there were no educational requirements for becoming a police officer. Anyone of "good character" could become a "policeman," a term that was used well into the 1980s.

James Griffin (who went on to become the first black Deputy Chief of Police) joined the St. Paul police force in 1941. That year, he reports that not everyone had a high school diploma. A few could barely write their names so they needed help with writing reports. A high school diploma became a requirement in January 1950. Civil Service examination scores were used for awarding promotions. With the exception of a high school diploma, requirements were not much different when Larry McDonald joined the force in 1955, fourteen years after Griffin. During both Griffin's and McDonald's careers, there was a growing emphasis on recruiting good people. Background checks and the licensure process were started.

In 1965, Congress passed the Law Enforcement Assistance Act to encourage police officers to attend college and earn a liberal arts degree. In 1968, the year of the riots at the Democratic Convention in Chicago, the act was amended so that institutions of higher learning could be reimbursed for teaching police officers who were enrolled in their law enforcement programs. St. Paul participated in the program in 1969.

Today, an applicant who wishes to become a police officer must have earned a two-year or four-year degree from a POST (Peace Officers Standards and Training Board) approved program in criminal justice or law enforcement. Since 1979, after completing the degree, the student is eligible to take the eight-week Skills Course, which consists of nine courses in the Professional Licensing Core (PLC)

offered by the Center for Criminal Justice and Law Enforcement in both St. Paul and Minneapolis. Firearms training and practice, as well as handcuffing, defensive driving, defensive tactics, suspect search, and traffic law are examples of subjects taught in this program. No student may be admitted to the PLC program if he or she has any history of criminal behavior.

About ten colleges offer approved law enforcement programs in the state of Minnesota. If an applicant already has a degree in a POST-approved course sequence in law enforcement or criminal justice, he or she can apply directly to the PLC. After completion of the degree and the PLC courses, the applicant must then pass the Minnesota Peace Officer Licensing Examination, which was initiated in 1984. When all of these requirements have been successfully completed, the graduate can then apply for the position of St. Paul police officer through the Police Department's Office of Human Resources. A background investigation, a psychological examination, and an oral examination are than completed. If successful, he or she is then placed on an "eligible for hire" list.

Those eligible for hire then attend the Police Academy for four months. There were 250 applications for the fall 2007 class. Fifty-six were accepted. The St. Paul Police Department is considered an outstanding department so there are almost always more applicants than spaces in upcoming classes. Forty-five students graduated on December 20, 2007. Twenty speak at least one other language besides English, six are women, and they range in age from 22 to 36.

The program is exhausting both physically and mentally. The students learn to rappel down a fire tower located in Energy Park. They are each given a Glock 22 gun and instructed on how to use it. They do military-style drills, run miles each day, and learn the importance of detailed report writing. They learn defensive tactics, building searches, interviewing skills, and detection of drunk drivers. After graduation from the academy, each officer is then paired with a field-training officer for 12 to 16 weeks to gain experience working the streets. After their field experience, each officer returns to the academy for several more weeks. The new officers then have a probationary period of one year.

Police work is often a family tradition. A family member entering the field is a so-called "legacy" applicant. There is a particularly high rate of success among these sons, daughters, nieces, brothers, and nephews of police officers because they know what the job entails. They also have realistic expectations and are proud to enter the law enforcement profession. Josh Lynaugh, son of Timothy Lynaugh, and Dan Ficcadenti, son of Mark Ficcadenti, are recent examples of this tradition. Both young men were in the fall 2007 class of the Police Academy and each received his father's badge at graduation.

The goal of police education is to teach officers how to stay safe and serve the citizens. Every effort is made to prepare a police officer for as many situations as possible. However, sometimes each one will be called upon to make a split-second decision in an unpredictable situation on the job. Perceptions and opinions about these split-second decisions in a particular situation may differ. As a result, a police officer can be vulnerable in the aftermath of a departmental review or a citizen complaint.

There is no short road to becoming and remaining a police officer in St. Paul. After satisfactorily completing all of the entrance requirements, officers stay current in their field by completing forty-five mandatory continuing education credits every three years. These credits must be approved by the P.D.I. (Professional Development Institute) of the department.

The department also wants their officers to stay fit physically. Every officer is expected to participate in a fitness program for three hours each week. They can do this on duty time. This is critical to their job performance and their own safety because officers may find themselves chasing fugitives on foot through all kinds of places and terrain.

For police officers wishing to become canine officers, there are additional things to be considered. First of all, they must have about three years of successful

Dan Ficcadenti receives his father Mark's badge upon graduating from the St. Paul Police Academy, December 20, 2007. Courtesy of the St. Paul Pioneer Press, *Sherri La Rose-Chiglo, photographer.*

Follow the Dog

experience on the job. Second, the family must be willing to welcome a new canine into the family. The home must be able to accommodate a large, energetic dog (no apartment dwellers here), and outdoor space for a kennel and exercise must be available. The applicant is questioned by an Interview Panel. The panel includes the Chief of Police or a Deputy Chief of Police, the K-9 Commander, the Canine Unit's Sergeant, the Head Trainer, and a union representative. Former handlers including a female and a person of color also participate.

Once a candidate is accepted, he or she will be assigned to a dog (more information about the dogs appears in Chapter Five). In St. Paul, two Basic Canine Handler School courses are held each year, one in the spring and one in the fall. The course lasts 12 weeks.

Mark Ficcadenti, the current Head Trainer, says that communication between the handler and the dog is the most important aspect of starting a successful canine team. It continues to be a critical element to long-term success throughout the team's career together. The handler must be consistent in giving clear, concise instructions to the dog. The dog is literal-minded and sees things as black or white. The handler must learn to be consistent in *all* aspects of working with the dog. That includes use of the

Waiting can be part of training as Larry Nevin and Duke show. Courtesy of Larry Nevin.

leash, use of one's voice, and inflection of one's voice. A dog will become confused if the handler's behavior is inconsistent.

A great deal of patience on everybody's part is essential. The dogs that are being trained today usually have not been socialized with people and most do not understand the English language. Because most come from rural European breeders, they have never experienced the sights and sounds of a city. They do not know that tile is slippery or that steps have different heights and treads. Many people tend to shout at another person when he or she does not hear or understand something. With the dogs, shouting can interfere with their learning. The dogs are very bright and they quickly pick up on negative as well as positive human responses to them.

The dogs have a great deal to learn and it takes time. An exhausted handler can lose patience. Ficcadenti and his five trainers have an important role in coaching the handlers and keeping them level-headed when interacting with their dogs.

During the first month of training, the teams walk 2 to 2½ miles twice a day. This conditions both the handlers and the dogs. Dogs learn basic obedience, which includes heel, sit, and other basic commands, during the same time. Control of the dog is essential to the safety of the handler, the dog, suspects, and the general public.

Weather can increase stress levels for everyone when less than idyllic conditions arise. For instance, the class that started August 13, 2007, experienced one of the worst and longest heat waves reported in Minnesota. For weeks, they started early, at 5:30 or 6 a.m. to avoid the hottest temperatures. Classes held in the late evening were not much better because nights seldom cooled off. The class that had started in the winter of that year had a very different problem. Then it was cold and there was deep snow, which is exhausting to navigate for both the handlers and the dogs.

Occasionally, a handler is unable to control his or her dog. This is usually due to a physical problem. The handler may be asked to leave and the dog is then reassigned to another officer. Most handler class members are in their late 20s and early 30s and should be able to keep up with the trainers who are mainly in their 50s. It does not take long for a handler to realize that his or her physical condition is a critical issue in becoming and remaining a canine handler.

The second and third month of training include more obedience work, agility work by the dog, getting used to the sound of gunfire, tracking human scent, searching buildings and open areas, and evidence search. In addition, dogs learn to chase and apprehend a fleeing person, to attack on command, and to protect their handler. There are also classes given by an emergency care veterinarian. Handlers learn how to do First Aid, including how to stem bleeding, apply bandages, and care for fractures and gun shot wounds, as well as how to perform CPR on their dogs.

One of the Canine Unit's newest teams is that of Nicole Rasmussen and her dog Chase, 2007. Courtesy of Nicole Rasmussen.

The May 2007 graduation class had one woman, Nicole Rasmussen, and her dog, Chase. She became the fifth female handler in the unit's history. She had thoroughly investigated what it would take to become a canine handler. In addition, she had trained her female German shepherd, Heidi, for Schutzhund, a rigorous dog sport with competition in tracking, obedience, and protection. Rasmussen did and does regular cardio conditioning and upper body strength conditioning exercises. She knows that her regular exercises not only keep her strong but they also make her less prone to injury. Rasmussen also commented that she has been able to fit in with an all-male group because of the leadership of Sergeant Paul Dunnom and Mark Ficcadenti.

Training methods have changed through the years. The biggest change in training is a much more positive approach toward the dog. Handlers use more incentives such as toys and food. In former years, force and pain were the primary means used to compel the dog into a desired behavior. Today, the emphasis is on positive rewards in a motivational training method.

Canine training takes place in a variety of settings. Midway Stadium, the Minnesota State Fair grounds, public schools, the old Hamm's brewery, the Timothy J. Jones Training Facility, and other available spaces have all been used.

Handler training is arduous and concentrated but after a team completes the course, dogs and handlers demonstrate what they have learned at graduation ceremonies held in front of peers, friends, families, and public figures, such as mayors and police chiefs. In 2007 graduation ceremonies were held in May and November at the Timothy J. Jones

$1.00 Donation

The United States Police K-9, Region 12
Presents a Public Demonstration
Of All The Finest K-9 Teams In The Country
Fri. August Tenth, 1979 7:30 PM
Harding High School 1540 E. Sixth Street, St. Paul, MN
Free Parking Harding Football Stadium

Demonstrations of police canine skills are often held for the public. Courtesy of the St. Paul Police Department.

Canine Training Facility. Three of the thirteen teams graduating in May were from St. Paul and one of the twelve teams graduating in November was from St. Paul. These numbers reflect the St. Paul Canine Unit's role in training teams from many other agencies.

Unfortunately, injuries can occur during training. Some are minor but some can be quite serious. When a dog comes running at full speed toward a handler playing the bad guy (wearing a padded sleeve), a dog will grab onto the sleeve and may swing around in such a way that the handler's knee is injured from behind. Lawrence Nevin was injured that way. He said the only fortunate part of this event was that his beloved Duke was getting old and needing to retire at the same time. Nevin became a trainer and was given a second dog but was transferred out of the unit in 1980 after seven years of service. Nevin was the Director of Audiovisual Services when he retired from the St. Paul Police Department in 1998.

Timothy Lynaugh was injured in a similar way. In 2006, after 12 years in the Canine Unit, he had to transfer out of the unit because of the severity of his knee injury. Lynaugh is currently an officer in Homeland Security and Special Events and he is working on a master's degree in Criminal Justice Administration. Lynaugh says, "I would go back to canine work in a heart beat and work for free if I could." Almost all of the retired and/or transferred officers express the same sentiment—they agree that their years with the Canine Unit were the best years of their careers.

Dogs that are trained for the Canine Unit are called all-purpose dogs. In addition to all-purpose training, dogs may be cross-trained to do an additional job. In shorter courses, a team may also learn to detect narcotics or explosives. Some dogs are single-purpose dogs such as Clancy, a chocolate Labrador retriever. Clancy and his handler work for Minnesota's Department of Natural Resources (DNR) where he is one of a very few dogs in the world that detects mercury. Other single-purpose dogs may become detectors of narcotics, explosives, or wildlife.

Minnesota's DNR is increasingly using dogs to detect illegal game and fish. They have had their own canine unit since 1990. Richard Hansen, a DNR conservation officer stationed in Duluth, worked with Poncho, the first fish and game tracking dog in the nation to be certified by the U.S. Police Canine Association. In 1999, when it was found that conservation officers were nine times more likely to be assaulted than police officers (because they were facing increased hard-core crimes like theft, drugs, and organized poaching in rural areas), the DNR began to use German shepherds instead of Labradors because it had become clear that there was a need for a dog that could protect its handler as well as identify fish and game. Detector dogs are trained in school buildings, office spaces, impound lots, rental car yards, and similar spaces.

In the last decade, the breadth of training activities at the Timothy J. Jones Canine Training Facility has grown in terms of the kinds of training activities and the wide variety of agencies it serves. It has truly become a canine training center serving a much broader community than just St. Paul.

Saint Paul Police Canine Graduation Ceremonies

May 24, 2007

John M. Harrington
Chief of Police

Graduation ceremonies are held in May and November of each year at the Timothy J. Jones Canine Training Facility. Courtesy of the author.

Chapter Five

The Remarkable Dogs

Successful development of the inherent capabilities of a dog gives a trainer, an owner, and a dog a sense of confidence and accomplishment. Innate traits of a particular breed dictate some of the end qualities desired for a particular job. For example, Labrador and golden retrievers make excellent guide dogs because of their intelligence, size, and disposition. For the same reasons and also because of their keen sense of smell, both breeds make excellent detector dogs. The German shepherd dog is almost a synonym for police dog. Throughout the world and for many decades, there has been agreement among people in police work that the German shepherd is the best-suited breed for that work. The Belgian Malinois may be used also. Some mixed breeds can be successful. Jon Sherwood's dog, Roscoe, for example, was part German shepherd and part Akita. Even when a particular breed is determined to be well suited for a particular job, it does not mean that every dog in the litter will be able to perform as a canine partner.

Dogs must be assessed for many factors before acceptance for police training. Temperament testing for police work involves the setting up of a series of situations to determine suitability for future performance on the job. Dogs are checked for a prey drive, intelligence, noise sensitivity, startle reflex, energy, strength, confidence, suitable aggressiveness, and courage. In addition, Mark Ficcadenti, the Head Trainer in St. Paul, identifies three kinds of drive that need to be assessed. The prey drive is the desire to catch a moving object; the defensive drive is the dog's ability to defend itself rather than run away; the fight drive is the willingness to apprehend and stay committed to the fight as needed. A comfortable dog has his tail up and wagging. Dogs with an avoidance of high stress situations are ruled out. After the temperament assessment, a veterinarian checks the dog for any

physical defects that might interfere with police work. Assessment of many dogs to find the right ones is a time-consuming job and therefore expensive because of lost manpower hours involved.

From the inception of the first St. Paul canine police work from 1958–61 and from 1972 to the early 2000s, all dogs were donated. They were given to the department by breeders and by owners. As canine work became more developed, some of the selection factors in temperament testing changed. James Cocchiarella, the first Head Trainer in St. Paul, was also a breeder of German shepherds. He looked for friendliness, an outgoing personality, and what he called the "fear factor." This was judged by the way a dog reacted when afraid. Did the dog retreat or stand pat? He also wanted a dog that had been socialized. The dog was then checked by a veterinarian.

As the St. Paul canine program grew, assessment took more and more of an officer's time. Out of ten dogs offered, maybe only one had the right qualities. It often took as long as three days to locate one dog suitable for canine training. Frequent appeals in the media— radio, newspaper, and television—were required to maintain even a minimum number of new dogs. Good dogs were getting more difficult to find. During the late 1990s, the inherent problems with donated dogs became apparent. First of all, American German shepherd breeders tended to breed show dogs and family pets, rather than concentrating on the qualities a dog needs to do police work. Secondly, because the dogs came at no cost, their perceived value was lessened. Finally, the officer's time taken for assessment was lost to the professional work of the unit.

It seemed time to look at importing dogs from elsewhere to obtain dogs that were bred to be police dogs. A few attempts to find dogs in the United States were unsuccessful and the dogs had to be sent back. The first dog imported from Europe was Ranger. He came from East Germany in 1996; James Decowski was his handler. European breeders tended to produce a more aggressive, courageous, and even more athletic dog.

After several frustrating experiences trying to buy dogs, the unit was determined to find a reputable vendor who could be counted on to assess a dog properly before it arrived. For the next four or five years, the unit advertised for dogs locally and also started obtaining dogs from Europe through dependable vendors. Frequently a private citizen or an organization donated money for the cost of an imported dog. Occasionally, a lively dog would be found at a dog pound. Unit personnel have saved more than one dog from euthanasia.

Today, the dogs cost $7,200. Dogs usually come from the rural areas of Germany, the Czech Republic, and Slovakia. They are assessed by the vendor before the dog is sent to St. Paul. All selected dogs are male. They are rarely neutered. Females tend to be overprotective of the handler and may break their concentration when tracking by returning to check on

Reggie demonstrates his ladder-climbing skills as his handler Glen Kothe watches. Courtesy of Glen Kothe.

Jumping barriers is easy for Duke as he and his handler Larry Nevin demonstrate. Courtesy of Larry Nevin.

the handler. Dogs need to be between one and two years old before they are trained. However, dogs mature at different ages.

Each new dog is matched with a handler who brings the dog home to become integrated into the handler's family. The handler gives the dog his name. Sometimes a family member thinks up the name and in some cases the handler starts a contest to name the dog. In most cases this is the dog's first socialization experience so it may take time to develop acceptable behavior with family members. Occasionally, a dog is so protective of his handler that he has problems engaging with other family members. However, a dog quickly learns that when his handler puts on the police uniform, he must jump in the car and go to work. The bonding with his handler grows with training together for twelve weeks, working together, and living together throughout the months and years. When a handler says, "That dog saved my life more times than I can count," it is clear that the two really learned to work as one.

The details of training were addressed in Chapter Four, but there are some aspects of training that apply only to the dog. The dog first learns obedience. Next the dog learns agility which involves crawling under places with low clearance, walking across open ladders, climbing ladders, and jumping over obstacles. A dog learns to apprehend only when he is released and only on the handler's command. A dog learns to take hold of the right arm and high on the body, as the impact of their weight above a person's waist is more likely to carry a person off his feet.

Crossing a horizontal ladder helps a dog learn agility. Courtesy of the St. Paul Police Department.

Dogs learn to search both on and off lead. When a dog locates a suspect in a building, he is taught to bark or alert the handler by his posture or stance. When this occurs in a real situation, the handler then gives the suspect a verbal warning, "St. Paul Police Canine Unit. Come out or I'll send the dog." Finally, the dog learns to protect his handler. However, this looks almost instinctive when you see one of these dogs concentrating on his handler's location and every move.

When Donald Slavik was Head Trainer, he said, "Even after the formal training period, it takes a long time for the two of you to get to know each other's moves and what the other will do under certain circumstances. However, once you get the team work down, it's really something." He added, "We don't take a dog that's got a record of biting." However, the dogs are taught acceptable aggression.

Slavik lists four rules for a handler in relation to his or her dog. First, love your dog. Second, be a good police officer. Third, make your dog a part of your life, and last, defend him as he defends you. Sherwood adds, "Once at home, the dog sheds the work ethic and gets down to the real business of eating, playing, and just lying around."

Maintaining the dog's health is critical. Nutrition and exercise are key. The dogs are like trained athletes. They must practice every day in order to maintain their skills and prevent injury. When a health problem arises, the Como Park Animal Hospital serves as the canine health care provider. The most common problems are sprains, strains, and soft tissue injuries in the line of duty. Open wounds are also common. In addition, idiopathic problems that have no known explanation may arise. In emergencies and when an immediate life-threatening situation arises, the handler brings the dog to the University of Minnesota Small Animal Hospital, which is a part of the College of Veterinary Medicine.

A dog's work career lasts about six to eight years depending on its general physical condition. Dogs have a hard time understanding retirement. When a dog's work skills decline or his health becomes fragile, he no longer goes to work with his handler, the person he has watched faithfully for years. The dog looks on wistfully when the handler puts on the uniform and walks out the door alone. Many handlers say that, even after months of retirement, their canine partners still look hopeful when they leave for work. When a dog's health deteriorates to the point that he must be put down, the distress is extraordinary for the handler as well as the family. Larry Nevin says that the hardest thing he ever had to do was to put down his beloved Duke. After working with Lobo for ten years, Don Martin reports, "I cried like a baby and I was not ashamed to do so" when Lobo was put down.

Four St. Paul canines have been killed in action. The shock of suddenly losing a constant companion that has saved your life on more than one occasion is almost unbearable.

The first dog to be killed in action was Radar, whose handler was Mark Klinge. They had worked together for six years. On May 20, 1982, the two were called at night to search for a burglar at the State Agriculture Building at 90 West Plato Boulevard. Radar picked up a scent that led them to the fourth floor where there was an open door. Radar shot through the door, which gave access to the roof. In the dark, Radar teetered on the edge, could not right himself, and fell over. Klinge ran downstairs, gave him CPR, but the dog died in his arms. Devastated, Klinge brought the dog home, woke up his family, and they buried Radar in the dog's favorite place in their backyard.

The second dog to be killed in action was Wojo, whose handler was Eugene Burke. In 1985, the dog had flushed out two suspected robbers from some deep grass at Minnehaha Avenue and McKnight Road. There were police helicopters in the air. Wojo continued his work. However, while Wojo was chasing the two men down the road, he was killed by a passing car.

Laser was killed along with his partner, Timothy Jones, on August 26, 1994. They were tracking a suspect who had killed another young police officer, Ron Ryan, Jr., in the morning. The full story of this tragedy is told in the next chapter.

The fourth dog, Callahan, was killed on May 25, 1998. His handler, Timothy Lynaugh, and Callahan were called to help homicide officers apprehend a murder suspect. It

Gene Burke and Wojo on the left and Tom Burke and Kojak on the right, 1983. Two years later Wojo was hit and killed by a car while the canine officer was chasing two would-be robbers. Courtesy of the St. Paul Police Department.

happened near Arcade and Minnehaha where children were playing in the yards, making the situation particularly precarious. Just as Lynaugh shouted, "Police officer with a dog. Come out," a bullet passed by his feet, but he was not sure where it came from. Callahan knew and ran in the bushes behind the garage where the man shot the dog, but not before the dog bit the suspect. When the suspect ran out of bullets, he yelled, "Don't shoot me." Lynaugh approached and found that the man had been lying down and shooting between his knees which explained why none of Lynaugh's shots was effective. Lynaugh then grabbed Callahan and took him to the University of Minnesota Small Animal Hospital, but it was too late. Tragically, Callahan had been shot in the head. Lynaugh ends his story, "Callahan saved my life."

Before Timothy Jones was killed, he had tended an area at the training center as a cemetery for the dog of any handler who wished to use it. There he had buried his first dog, Ninja. Other officers' dogs were buried there also. After Jones and Laser were killed, an anonymous St. Paul woman wanted to turn this cemetery into a special memorial to the animals. She was able to persuade Larry Kelly, Vice President of Field Operations at Kraus-Anderson, a construction company, and Terry Anderson at BWBR Architects to donate the design and construction of a beautiful area with a winding wooded pathway not far from the kennels. There is a black wrought iron fence with a gate at the entrance. Each grave has a marker and there is a statue of a German shepherd overlooking the graves. Markers honor both of Timothy Jones' dogs, Ninja and Laser, although both dogs were buried with Jones.

The entrance to the St. Paul Police Canine Cemetery is next to the Timothy J. Jones Canine Training Facility in Maplewood, Minnesota. Courtesy of the author.

A statue of a German shepherd, often the Canine Unit's preferred breed, guards the cemetery at the Timothy J. Jones Training Facility. Courtesy of the author.

Bricks honoring St. Paul Canine Unit dogs at the Nestlé Purina Memories Garden on the University of Minnesota St. Paul campus. Courtesy of the author.

There is one other place that honors the four St. Paul Police dogs killed in action. It is the Nestlé Purina Memories Garden behind the University of Minnesota Small Animal Hospital. It was established in 2002 to provide a private, outdoor place for pet owners who have lost a dog. Wrought iron benches stand among the plants and bushes. Brick pavers commemorate pets that have died. The inscribed bricks are purchased through the College of Veterinary Medicine Social Work Service, which provides support, advocacy, and referral services to clients dealing with issues related to their companion animals' health, wellness, and death. There is a brick for each of the St. Paul dogs killed in action—Radar, Wojo, Laser, and Callahan. There are also three bricks commemorating the three Minneapolis police dogs that met a similar fate. The love from and for these remarkable dogs is boundless. The following words try to express the depth of this love. The words are found in many publications about police dogs but this writer was unable to find the author.

The Police Dog

My eyes are your eyes
To watch and protect you and yours.

My ears are your ears
To hear and detect evil minds in the dark.

My nose is your nose
To scent the invader of your domain.

And so you may live
My life is also yours.

Chapter Six

Officer Down

"Officer down!" When a dispatcher speaks those dreaded words, it mobilizes any police force with greater energy and emotion than any other words possibly could. It had been 24 years since a St. Paul police officer had been killed in the line of duty. Then on the morning of Friday, August 26, 1994, those ominous words were heard across the St. Paul police radios.

It all began at 7 a.m. One hour before going off duty, Ron Ryan, Jr., a 26-year-old rookie officer, took a "slumper" call to check on a man reportedly sleeping in a red car in the parking lot outside the Sacred Heart Catholic Church on St. Paul's East Side. Ryan found Guy Harvey Baker asleep. Ryan woke Baker, took his identification, including a passport, and walked back to his squad car to do a routine check. Baker, 26 years old, became alarmed that the officer would find out that he had an outstanding arrest warrant in Iowa and that the red car might have been reported stolen. The fearful Baker took a 38-caliber revolver that he had hidden in his lap and shot Ron Ryan, Jr., several times, twice in the head. Baker quickly ran to check on Ryan and turned him over to see if he was still alive. When he found no response, he grabbed the officer's revolver and ran to his car, which at first would not start. So he pushed it down a slight incline and managed to get it started. He drove away in the red car at high speed, but not before a neighbor who had witnessed the encounter got out his own gun and shot out the back window of the fleeing car. Other neighbors heard the shots and called 911. In Baker's haste to get away, he did not notice that his passport was under Ryan's body. Because of this error, the police knew who they were looking for and what he looked like.

Officers came from everywhere to begin the search. Because this incident occurred just before 8 a.m., there was one shift of police going off duty and another shift coming on duty. Members of both shifts joined in the

manhunt. By the end of the day Chief of Police William Finney said at least four SWAT teams, involving over one hundred officers from St. Paul, Minneapolis, several surrounding suburbs, the State Patrol, and the State Bureau of Criminal Apprehension, had participated in the operation. In addition, Governor Arne Carlson sent a 125-member National Guard police unit to provide flak jackets, helmets, and night vision goggles. Police helicopters were quickly in the air.

Officer Tim Jones, a 16-year veteran of the police department and member of the Canine Unit, was at home with his children that morning. When he received a call about Ryan, he took his children to day care, got his German shepherd, Laser, and joined in the manhunt. In the meantime, the red car was found abandoned in the parking lot of the Johnson Brothers Liquor Store at 1165 Old Hudson Road. Two young boys reported that they saw the suspect run north into a nearby wooded area. Afterward, Baker reported that he made circular trails and poured lighter fluid on the ground to confuse any dogs he knew would be called to hunt him down.

At around 10 a.m., Laser picked up Baker's scent. Laser led Jones and other officers to an ice fishing house on a skid behind the garage at 1124 Conway. The house had a padlock on the door and no floor. Baker had managed to crawl inside from underneath the shack. A strip of plexiglas all the way around it gave him a way to watch the officers approach. Laser stopped and signaled that he had found his man. Hearing sounds outside, Baker looked out the window, saw Tim Jones, and shot him. A few seconds later, Baker ran from the shack and Laser attacked him. According to Kristin von Kreisler's book *The Compassion of Animals*, when Laser first bit Baker's leg, Baker shot the dog. Laser, although bleeding, grabbed Baker's leg a second time and was shot again. Laser collapsed but was still able to crawl toward Baker. One more shot killed the dog. Both Jones and Laser were shot in the head. The intensive search continued.

The police cordoned off blocks of area houses. SWAT teams went from house to house telling residents to stay inside their homes. Just before 1 p.m., officers found Baker hiding under a piece of plywood leaning against the house at 1129 Euclid Street. For unknown reasons, Baker had put his own gun and the guns of both officers under the deck of a neighboring house. He was dressed in camouflage with his face covered with camouflage netting. He said little on the way to the hospital where he was checked, treated for dog bites and other minor scrapes, and then taken to jail. Personnel at the hospital said they had never seen such a high level of security. There were at least a dozen officers guarding him. When Baker finally arrived at the jail, it was about 1:30 p.m. The manhunt was over. Shock and grief were about to take hold.

Twenty-six-year-old Ron Ryan, Jr., had been the first officer down. Son of a police officer, he grew up on the East Side of St. Paul and often worked there. After high school,

Ron worked for four years as a parking-enforcement officer. He then took the police test, passed, and enrolled in the academy to become a police officer. He had always wanted to follow in his father's footsteps. He had been a proud police officer for only a year, earning two commendations in that short time. At Ron's funeral, Chief of Police Finney said in a broken voice, "Ron Ryan, Jr., was one of the best young police officers this department has ever seen. In only a few short months, he made this department very proud." Ron had been married just a year, leaving his wife, Ann, a widow at age 28. He was also survived by his parents, a sister, both grandmothers, Ann's parents, and her brother's family.

The second officer down was 36-year-old Timothy Jones whose canine partner, Laser, also died. Jones was survived by his wife Roxanne, nine-year-old son Matthew, seven-year-old daughter Chelsey, three sisters, and members of Roxanne's family. Tim was a 1975 graduate of Harding High School where he excelled in football, baseball, and wrestling. He remained an athlete, playing both shortstop and outfield on the St. Paul Police softball team as well as on the all-star group of police ballplayers (the Twin City Lawmen). Tim and his wife had moved into their new "dream" house just three years prior to his death. Their neighbors reported that he was a wonderful father and valued neighbor. He was also very conscientious about practicing commands with his dogs on a

Members of the Critical Incident Response Team prepare to check Conway Street in search of the suspect in the shooting of Officer Ron Ryan, Jr., 1994. Courtesy of the St. Paul Pioneer Press, *Joe Oden, photographer.*

regular basis. He had been with the St. Paul Police Department for 16 years and had been in the Canine Unit since 1989.

Officer Jones had received many commendations and awards from competitions. His commendations included helping to rescue elderly residents from a burning apartment building (July 1992), capturing four auto theft suspects (February 1993), and arresting a suspect who had fled from the Minneapolis police (June 1994).

He also won awards in national canine competitions. In 1988, the St. Paul Police Department's team placed second in a six-state competition at Superior, Wisconsin. Jones also placed fifth in overall competition categories of the U.S. Police Canine Association's Region 18 Certification Trials. In 1989, the department took top honors competing against the nation's top eleven teams at Greenwood Village, Colorado. Jones, known as Nipper to his friends, and his dog Ninja took third place in the individual competition. In 1990, the unit ranked first among 160 officer-dog teams at Dunedin, Florida, where Jones and Ninja also won awards in individual categories.

Jones' fellow officers found several ways of coping with this horrific loss. They got together, traded stories, and helped prepare for the funerals. They polished Tim's boots and buttons to a shiny gloss. As soon as one friend put down a sparkling button, another would pick it up and give a sharp rebuke, "Ain't shiny enough." They even polished his famous belt buckle (a pig), which made fun of uncomplimentary notions about cops. They did all this in

Police squad cars formed a funeral procession from the Cathedral of St. Paul to Roselawn Cemetery in Roseville, for the burial of Tim Jones, 1994. Courtesy of the St. Paul Pioneer Press, *John Doman, photographer.*

Officer Pat Lyttle's kitchen. Jones had been a mentor and teacher for many rookies. He was a cop's cop and a vital part of the close-knit Canine Unit. There had been a foursome on the night shift: Jon Sherwood, Russ Garvey, Tom Bergren, and Jones. The remaining three and other Night Fighters served as pallbearers for Jones. Not surprising, the dogs in the unit were reported to be on edge, anxious, and very aware of the tensions of their handlers.

Jones had had his second dog, Laser, for only two years. Ninja was the dog with whom he had won honors in four national trials and was part of a Canine Department roster that was cited three times as the top in the country. Jones had been devastated when Ninja died. He had had the dog cremated and then placed the ashes in an urn that he kept in the trunk of his car for almost six months. He occasionally asked people, "Want to see my dog?" Very few took up his offer. Eventually, Jones picked up a nice piece of sod from a landscaping project at his house and took it and the urn to the special cemetery for canine partners he had started at the training center. He carefully buried Ninja. Before the funeral, Jones' friends went to the cemetery and dug up a cooler that held Ninja's urn. They found that it was dated, labeled, and contained a note, "Gone, but not Forgotten." His friends brought the urn to the casket so that both his dogs, Ninja and Laser, could be buried with him.

Mourners came from everywhere: neighbors, strangers, local police, and friends from other states and other countries. Mayor Norm Coleman remarked, "St. Paul has lost part of its heart and soul today. The extent of the tragedy is unfathomable." Governor Arne Carlson ordered all flags flown at half-mast until after both funerals. Usually the Canine Unit presented public demonstrations during the Minnesota State Fair. But this year, with the deaths occurring during Fair time, all programs were cancelled. Members of the public brought food and flowers to police stations and offered their prayers. At the East Side precinct, strangers dropped off plates of food for the officers who were working double shifts and for those coming in on their days off. One note to the Ryan and Jones families read, "We offer you our sympathy at your loss, and that of the entire community." Flowers filled the police headquarters lobby. When the emergency room doctors who cared for the officers tried to describe the extent of their injuries, they wept. Condolences to the family, friends, and colleagues came from around the United States, Scotland, England, and Canada. A constable in Lincolnshire, England, expressed what people at a distance felt, "No matter where it happens, it is always a loss to us all."

Visitation for Ronald Ryan, Jr., was on Monday afternoon. On Tuesday morning, there were prayers at the Wulff Family Services Mortuary and the Mass of Christian Burial at Presentation of the Blessed Virgin Mary Church was followed by his interment at Union Cemetery. The day of the funeral service began at 8:30 a.m. when officers, under strict instructions about the limited church seating, turned away some early arrivals. One woman protested, "We're with the Ryan family." Officer Mike Schwab said, "Everyone who came in told us they were friends of the Ryan family." At 9:30, the doors opened to their friends and 2,000 police officers. Bagpipers played outside as an additional 2,000 mourners, all of them law enforcement officers, stood at attention. They were from Chicago, Des Moines, Polk County, and Mason City, Iowa, which was also the hometown of Guy Harvey Baker, the confessed killer. The officers stood erect with impassive faces in lines eight deep. Other mourners were able to express their grief more openly. They wept. Everyone watched as Ron's widow, Ann, came to the church door. This bride of a year took a deep breath, looked heavenward, and entered the church. After the mass, the procession of squad cars with their flashing lights stretched for miles. They passed a route lined with neighbors and children. Many waved flags and some held signs reading "God bless officers Ron Ryan and Tim Jones." Men held hats over their hearts and Boy Scouts stood at attention. Rows of men and women in blue uniforms protected the Ryans at the cemetery. The farewell ritual was the same for each officer as he or she filed by the casket. Each one doffed his or her cap and brushed their fingers along the polished wood. Ron's mother cried, placed a rose on top of the coffin, which she then hugged, and said, "He's supposed to be home with Annie."

Catching their breath, the mourners moved on to the visitation for Timothy Jones at the Bradshaw Adam Funeral Home that same afternoon. One officer talked about Jones and how he was known to stay at a crime scene when other officers had left. "He stayed with his dog until the suspect would come out." Even people who knew neither man came to the visitation. Robert Hill was among them. He had been inadvertently considered a possible accomplice. His home on the East Side had been tear-gassed on Friday, his dog shot, and he had been arrested during the search. The police helped him when they discovered their mistake. In spite of all this, he came. "I just wanted to pay my respects," said Hill. Jones and Laser had been shot in his yard.

The next day the Mass of Christian Burial was said for Jones at the St. Paul Cathedral. Hundreds of police officers did on Wednesday for Tim Jones what they had done on Tuesday for Ron Ryan, Jr., For blocks, squad cars with flashing lights lined the streets around the Cathedral. The procession of hundreds of cars went this time to Roselawn Cemetery in Roseville where Jones was buried with his beloved dogs. "Tim will always be part of us," was heard many times.

The grief of the last six days would now become more private. The department offered counseling to any officer requesting it.

Who was the perpetrator who changed so many lives? His name was Guy Harvey Baker. Like Ryan, Baker was 26 years old. He came from Mason City, Iowa, and had served in the Marines during the Persian Gulf War. He had learned to fire a short burst, assess the situation, and then resume shooting "until the threat is removed." He also must have been a "crack shot" or he could not have taken such accurate aim at the heads of both officers and the dog. He had been honorably discharged from the Marines. However, he had chronic back pain and other ailments associated with what is known as gulf war syndrome. Veterans link this problem with exposure to chemical agents during Operation Desert Storm. Prior to coming to Minnesota, Baker had been arrested for speeding and possession of pot and illegal firearms in Iowa. He was said to have a chip on his shoulder against the government and held a special hatred of cops. When he was finally arrested, he showed no remorse and said that he was "going to get them before they got me" and that he "would have shot more officers if he had had the means." Baker was charged under the 1989 Minnesota "heinous crime" statute which carries a "life without parole" sentence for killing a police officer. He confessed to the murders and is serving two consecutive life sentences at Oak Park Heights maximum-security prison where he is an education tutor, helping students in the prison educational system.

Ten years after these tragic events, a candlelight vigil in memory of the officers was held at the Minnesota Peace Officers Memorial on the State Capitol Mall. During those years, the officers' families had been rebuilding their lives. Ann Ryan, never forgetting her husband Ron, had remarried and has two small children. Roxanne Jones has been busy raising her two children—Matthew entered the University of St. Thomas in the fall of 2004 and Chelsey was still in high school. In 1997, the canine training center was renamed the Timothy J. Jones Canine Training Facility. That horrific day in 1994 will never be forgotten by anyone who knew and loved the two officers, Ron Ryan, Jr., and Timothy Jones.

The memorial where the candlelight vigil took place was dedicated in 1995, the year after the deaths of Ryan, Jones, and Laser. Designed by Fred Richter, its marble monument was originally placed at the Minneapolis-St. Paul International Airport in 1977. A lighted blue line leads from an archway to the marble slab, which is bathed in a continuous stream of water when weather permits. In the marble are carved the words from Matthew 5:9, "Blessed are the peacemakers for they shall be called the children of God." Along with both corporate and public contributions, police officers contributed heavily to help fund this memorial. Next to the monument, there is a stone tablet which reads in part:

> The blue line, which illuminates brightly at night, represents the 'thin blue line,' terminology often used when making reference to peace officers. Peace officers must walk that thin blue line daily as they protect democracy from anarchy, the lawful from the lawless, and order from chaos. Peace officers must walk that line to protect us from the worst impulses of society. This design is a tribute to the thin blue line of protection provided to us by our peace officers.

Chapter Seven

Recognition and Awards

The U.S. Police Canine Association (USPCA), the organization that sets professional standards, is the major source of recognition and awards for police canine units. The USPCA provides certification for canine teams in the areas of Patrol, Tracking, and all phases of Detector (narcotics, explosives, accelerants, wildlife, and cadavers). Certification of trainers and judges is also available through the USPCA.

Every year the USPCA sponsors seminars, certification of teams, and national field trials for outstanding performance. Certification takes place at the regional level. Region 18 includes Minnesota, Wisconsin, North Dakota, and Iowa. An individual handler/dog team with a score of 490 points out of a possible 700 will be certified. However, a team must be certified with a total score of 560 points or more to be eligible to compete at the annual national field trials. About 85 to 100 competitors and between 70 and 80 law enforcement agencies are represented at the annual national competitions. They may include teams from Canada, the CIA, the Secret Service, Homeland Security, police and sheriff's departments, and others from throughout the United States. The national competition was held in St. Paul in 1979 and 2006.

The USPCA National Field Trials Award for the #1 Department Canine Team in the United States went to the St. Paul Police Canine Unit in 1989, 1990, 1991, 1994, 1995, 1997, and 2000. The first team that won this distinction in 1989 included Officer Tim Jones and Ninja, Officer Paul Rhodes and Max, Officer Mike O'Brien and Rocky, Officer Dave Boll and Rondo, Officer Pat Lyttle and Shadow, and Officer Greg Majors and Sampson.

In 1995, the USPCA renamed the #1 Department Canine Team Award as the Timothy Jones/Laser Award. It was particularly gratifying that St. Paul won that year. It is reported that the St. Paul team adopted the motto, "Failure is not an option!" The 1995 winning team included Officer Dave Boll and Rondo, Officer Mark Ficcadenti and Tyke, Officer Russ Garvey and Boone, Officer Mark Sletner and Alex, Officer Jon Sherwood and Roscoe, and Officer Jim Long and Logan.

Follow the Dog

Pat Lyttle and Shadow pose in front of the Minnesota State Capitol with some of the USPCA awards won in 1989. Courtesy of the St. Paul Police Department.

Greg Majors and Sampson were part of the Canine Unit that won national top team honors in 1989. Courtesy of the St. Paul Police Department.

Jon Sherwood and his partner Roscoe, a German shepherd/Akita mix, were part of the national championship team in 1995. Three years later they won a national individual title. Courtesy of A. J. Forliti, photographer.

Russ Garvey and Boone won a national individual championship in 1995. Here the team is shown with Garvey's son Ray, then aged six. Courtesy of A. J. Forliti, photographer.

Dave Boll and Rondo won individual national championships in 1992 and 1993. Courtesy of A. J. Forliti, photographer.

The USPCA #1 Dog National Champion award was won by Officer Dave Boll and Rondo in both 1992 and 1993. In 1995, this award was won by Officer Russ Garvey and Boone. Garvey and Boone also won the Cahill Award for the highest total points in Obedience and Apprehension that same year. Jon Sherwood and Roscoe received the #1 Dog Champion award in 1998.

Other organizations occasionally honor either a person or a dog for excellent performance in a special situation. An example is the King Memorial Award. King was the first and most decorated police dog in Anoka County, serving from February 1967 to January 1975. His statue (by sculptor Rodger Brodin) is located in King Memorial Park in Anoka, Minnesota. In 1978, Radar received this award for protecting his handler, Officer Mark Klinge, when he was attacked by a man with a knife.

The William O. Stillman Award is another such example. It started in 1900 and is given by the Humane Society of the United States to people who risk their lives to save animals from danger and to animals that face danger to save the lives of people. In 1995, the award was given posthumously to Laser for his efforts to defend his partner, Timothy Jones.

The St. Paul Police Department awards the Medal of Valor Class A, the Medal of Merit Class B, and the Medal of Commendation Class C. It also gives an Officer of the Year Award,

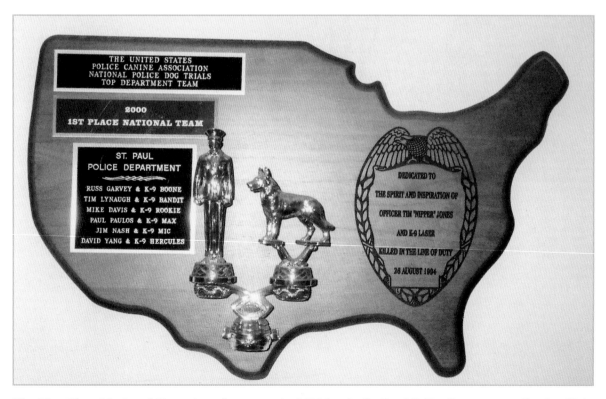

The First Place National Team Award was won in 2000 by the St. Paul Police Department Canine Unit. Courtesy of the St. Paul Police Department.

unit citations for exceptional performance, and letters of recognition for intelligent and excellent performance of regular duties.

The Medal of Valor Class A is awarded to a department member who, "conscious of danger, intelligently and in the line of police duty, distinguishes himself by the performance of an act of gallantry and valor at imminent personal hazard to life above and beyond the call of duty." While assigned to the Asian Gangs Unit, former canine handler officer Archie Smith received the Medal of Valor on August 8, 1993, "for his bravery and dedication while off duty, in rescuing a small child from drowning in a pond near his home and diligently searching for another child in the same pond."

On August 26, 1994, Officer Timothy Jones received the Medal of Valor award posthumously "for his ultimate sacrifice, and that of K-9 Laser who were searching in an off-duty status for the killer of Officer Ronald Ryan, Jr. They were ambushed by the same suspect and the wounds suffered were fatal." Officer Ronald Ryan, Jr., received the Medal of Valor posthumously on the same day for answering a "slumper" call when he was fatally wounded.

The Medal of Merit Class B is awarded for a highly creditable, unusual police accomplishment. After his canine assignment, Commander Laurence McDonald

As a member of the USPCA, St. Paul's canine unit has often competed in regional and national tests. This wall illustration is found at the Timothy Jones Training Facility. Courtesy of the author.

received this award "for his dedication to duty and outstanding performance in handling the department's response to Operation Rescue" during the summer of August 1993. This involved ensuring peaceful demonstrations at the Planned Parenthood Clinic on Ford Parkway.

On May 26, 1998, Officer Timothy Lynaugh, along with Sergeant Charles Anderson, Sergeant Neil Nelson, and Sergeant Richard Muñoz received the Medal of Merit "for courage and dedication in effecting the arrest of four murder suspects. The officers were clearly in harm's way. Officer Lynaugh's K-9, Callahan, was shot and killed by one of the suspects."

The Medal of Commendation Class C is given in "recognition for excellent performance of self-initiated police duties." Canine officers David Boll, Eugene Burke, Paul Dunnom, David Pavlak, Donald Slavik, and Timothy Jones all have received this honor.

The USPCA also gives a Medal of Valor award. Donald Bulver and his dog, Baron, received this Medal of Valor in1974. At the Minnehaha Bowling Lanes, a mentally unstable son of a police officer was waving a loaded gun around in the presence of several people. When the police arrived, the young man pointed the gun at the police officers. As Bulver released Baron, the young man shot Baron in the top of his head, grazing his skull. Knocked down and with a concussion, Baron continued to try to attack the man. Bulver then delivered a non-lethal shot that stopped the attacking man. After going on sick leave for a while, Baron recovered from his concussion and went back to work.

The USPCA recognizes canine teams in another way. It receives reports of outstanding canine police work from its members across the United States. It then recognizes one outstanding case each quarter and annually. Because St. Paul Police Canine teams have earned this distinction so often, only selected examples can be included here. Also included are a few cases that illustrate additional kinds of situations the canine teams encounter on a regular basis.

USPCA Case of the Year, 1998 – Officer Bradley Schultz and K-9, Tucker, were called to investigate a suspicious person. When Officer Schultz did a "pat" search, he found a hard, long object in the person's jacket. The suspect resisted violently and pulled out the object, a short-barreled shot gun. Schultz quickly drew his firearm, and released Tucker by hitting his squad car's bail-out door opener. As the man raised his shot gun at Schultz, Tucker took the suspect to the ground. Tucker saved Officer Schultz's life and enabled the suspect to be taken into custody without deadly force.

National Patrol Case of 1st Quarter, 2001 – Officer David Pavlak and his dog, Buster, were called to assist the Ramsey County Sheriff's Department at a drug dealer's home. When they knocked at the door, the suspect answered the door but then slammed it shut. The officers were able to clear the house of other people and then entered, giving the K-9 warning before Buster searched the first floor. They repeated this procedure on each floor until they arrived at the basement. There, Buster scratched at a locked door that had to be forced open because the suspect refused to come out. The man, armed with a screwdriver, was combative. Buster grabbed the man's left arm and dragged him out of the corner of the room. Buster held his bite while four officers were needed to secure the suspect. After the incident, Pavlak saw that Buster had been stabbed in the back, although he had shown no sign of injury while he did his work. Buster was treated for a one-inch puncture wound, a three-inch cut, and two small abrasions on his back. Fortunately, his wounds healed and he returned to work after his sick leave.

December 27, 2002 – Officer Brady Harrison and his dog, Justice, tracked an armed suspect for blocks through a densely populated urban area over grass, cement, and asphalt. Finally, Justice stopped and inhaled deeply at the bottom of a fence. When Harrison checked the other side of the fence, he found the discarded handgun, which was vital evidence in charging the person who was arrested later. The removal of a loaded gun from a densely populated area where children played may also have saved other lives.

National Finalist Patrol Case, 2004 – The Critical Incident Response Team (a disciplined unit of volunteer officers who respond to events that require special skills critical to preserving the safety of citizens and fellow officers in threatening and aggressive situations) and Mark Ficcadenti with his dog, Shadow, (one of a select few K-9 teams trained and deployed with the C.I.R.T.) were called to help in the apprehension of a barricaded suspect during a high-risk search warrant. Negotiations failed as the suspect, wanted for criminal sexual conduct, made irrational demands, so a tactical resolution was initiated. The power and gas to the house were shut off. The house was then tear-gassed but the man still refused to come out. After 45 minutes, a forced entry was made, and "flash bangs" were thrown into each room. Shadow overcame all the environmental distractions and found the man at the end of a long hallway. The suspect refused to comply with warning orders and fought with Shadow. However, Shadow kept the man engaged until several officers were able to take the man into custody.

National Case of the Quarter, 2004 – Officer John Buchmeier, his dog Ike, and Jason Brodt and his dog, Nitro, were called to a chaotic scene at the Warehouse Nightclub where a shooting had just occurred. Joining the officers already on the scene, the group coordinated their efforts to find a runaway man said to be wearing a white t-shirt. Buchmeier recruited a cover officer and with Ike immediately began tracking the suspect from the parking lot. Ike led them south of the building, across a lumber yard parking lot, and past another building where they found the man's white shirt. When they arrived at the lumber yard fence, Buchmeier knew that Brodt and Nitro were in a better position to enter the yard. Next, Brodt, two cover officers, and Nitro climbed the fence and Nitro was released to search the stacks of lumber. After about ten minutes, Brodt heard a loud cry from Nitro and feared for his life. Some minutes later they found Nitro holding the suspect's right leg, but not before the suspect had hit Nitro with a piece of lumber. The suspect dropped the board when he saw the officers, and thankfully Nitro was not seriously injured. The coordinated efforts of two canine teams led to a successful apprehension.

National Patrol Case of the 2nd Quarter, 2006 – As officers arrived at a home on Marion Street where an armed robbery had taken place, four suspects fled on foot. Officer Mike Davis and his K-9 partner, Rookie, arrived, coordinated a perimeter, and began an on-lead track of the suspects. Rookie took Davis along nearby railroad tracks, through woods, and down several blocks. A neighbor reported that a suspect was on the other side of the tracks where Rookie quickly continued, going around a broken fence, and across several more yards until they came to wet footprints in the grass. Rookie became frantic after arriving at a house in the next block. Davis spotted the suspect on the roof of the house as Rookie tried to climb the walls of the home. Officer Davis secured the house with his back-up and the suspect surrendered.

Officer Mark Blumberg and K-9, Cobra, were called over an hour later to a nearby area where another suspect was presumed to be hiding. Cobra took up a scent that took him across yards, down railroad tracks, and to some clothing discarded by the suspect. Continuing on, they saw a car driving slowly down the alley where a young woman jumped

The unit displays a trophy. From left to right are Dale Kangas and Butch, Chuck Geyer and Boss, Chief William McCutcheon, Deputy Chief John C. Nord, Tim Poucher and Prince, and Eugene Burke and Wojo. Courtesy of the St. Paul Police Department.

into the driver's seat. The suspect failed to comply with the commands of cover officers, threw the woman out of the car, moved behind the wheel, and locked himself in the car. Back-up officers provided cover for Blumberg while he smashed the driver's side window. As the suspect tried to get out of the car on the passenger side, Cobra was deployed into the car. Cobra apprehended the suspect while the officers were able to remain in positions of cover.

January 9, 2008 – Officer Nick Kellum and his K-9 partner, Juda, were called to assist the Minnesota Gang Strike Force for a narcotics search of a car. The officers had searched the car and found nothing. Kellum and Juda began an exterior search of the car. Juda indicated the presence of a narcotic odor when he began scratching and biting at the seam of the passenger door. Juda then went over the car's interior and he again gave his positive alert in the same area but inside the passenger door. Kellum found a small baggie of methamphetamine stuck between the plastic seat molding and the cushion. As a result of this find, the Gang Strike Force investigators obtained a search warrant for the car owner's house. When the warrant was executed, five people were arrested on narcotics charges, one for auto theft, and seven were identified as gang members (one was previously unknown as a gang member). There were also three stolen cars, two stolen motorcycles, suspected stolen electronic equipment, firearms, ammunition, narcotics paraphernalia, and six more ounces of methamphetamine. The resulting felony arrests and recovery of stolen property came as the result of Juda's find.

This sampling of reported cases gives a glimpse into the day-to-day work of the St. Paul Police Canine Unit. Few of us are aware of the intelligence, the training, the patience, the strategic planning, and courage required for this special police work. Each incident underscores the importance of the handler/dog teams to the successful resolution of the cases. There is a brass plaque for each of the unit's award-winning cases. The plaques are displayed on a wall at the Timothy J. Jones Training Facility. USPCA trophies are displayed in cabinets in the same building.

Chapter Eight

The St. Paul Police Canine Unit Today

"The mission of the Saint Paul Police Department Canine Unit is to provide highly trained canine officer teams who serve, in a timely and professional manner, both the officers of the Saint Paul Police Department and the citizens of the City of St. Paul," (Canine/Mounted Police Unit Web site).

The present St. Paul Police Canine Unit includes 21 men, 1 woman, and 22 dogs. Fifteen members of the unit come from families who have served or now serve in the St. Paul Police Department. For example, there have been one or more members of the Renteria family with the St. Paul Police Department since 1949. Mike Ernster's great-uncle served for 49 years (1920–69). Jon Sherwood's great-great grandfather was killed in action. Besides other family members in police work, David Pavlak's wife, Catherine (the second female dog handler), now works in Predatory Offender Tracking in St. Paul. Without identifying all of the family connections of this group of officers, it is clear that many members of the present Canine Unit have a proud heritage of work in law enforcement.

The 22 teams of the St. Paul Police Canine Unit are under the direct supervision of a Sergeant. Sergeant Paul Dunnom has held this assignment since 2005. He is responsible for the day-to-day activities of the unit, which include scheduling of officer work hours, scheduling monthly in-service training of the teams, evaluating of officers, and maintenance of statistics for the unit.

There is a protocol used for determining appropriate requests for the service of a canine team. Whenever a team is called to go out on a job, the officer must submit a written log of the occurrence. The following is a summary of those logs for the year 2007:

★ The teams responded to approximately 26,000 requests for service.

★ The teams were deployed on 3,432 calls for such things as building searches, tracks for suspects and missing persons, open area searches, evidence searches, narcotics searches, and explosive sweeps.

★ The teams made 71 physical apprehensions of criminal suspects.

★ The teams made 862 Presence Arrests, which means that the suspect surrendered because of the presence of the dog.

★ Approximately 90 pounds of narcotics were located by the unit's teams and approximately 270 additional pounds of narcotics were recovered by single purpose dogs assigned to the Force Unit and the Narcotics Unit. This was mainly marijuana and amphetamine.

In addition, the staff ran two 12-week all-purpose canine courses, one narcotics course, and one explosives course. The trainers also trained trainers for other agencies. This is done during training courses when they work alongside Head Trainer, Mark Ficcadenti, and his four assistant trainers: Jason Brodt, Mike Davis, Dave Pavlak, and Jon Sherwood.

Dunnom reports that he receives four or five telephone calls each week from persons who want to donate an obstreperous pet to the unit. The fact is that the unit can often use lively retrievers as single purpose detector dogs. If a detector class is about to begin, Dunnom will ask the owner to bring the dog in for an evaluation of its behavior and temperament. A detector dog needs to have a strong drive, high energy, and curiosity. If the dog meets these standards, it will be accepted for training and live at the Timothy J. Jones Training Facility for a brief time until the dog is matched with a handler. If the dog is not successful during training, it is returned to the owner.

The St. Paul Canine Unit works and trains with other canine units in the United States, several state agencies, the Royal Canadian Mounted Police, and federal agencies such as the Bureau of Alcohol, Tobacco, and Firearms (ATF). Personnel in the unit share training ideas and pertinent experiences with other units, agencies, and colleagues on a regular basis.

Sergeant Dunnom has another important responsibility: namely, screening of applicants for handler training before an individual is interviewed by the entire panel of administrators and peers. When an opening for a position in the Canine Unit is posted, there are often 30 or more applicants. An applying officer must have a history of making good job decisions under stress. He or she must also have shown evidence of self motivation. Good physical health is important because working as a handler can exacerbate an existing health problem such as a bad back. Applicants must also be willing to work extra time with their dogs: such as exercising them, practicing their skills, and bathing and grooming them. The applicant's living environment and family are both part of a successful canine team.

The week of October 7, 2007, was, on the face of it, a typical week for the 22 teams of the St. Paul Police Canine Unit. Head Trainer Mark Ficcadenti and his assistant trainers were in their tenth week of intensive training of twelve officers with their new young dogs. Only one of the twelve teams was from the St. Paul Canine Unit. One trainee was a woman from Iowa, ten were from Minnesota police or sheriff's offices throughout the state and one was from the Minnesota Correctional Facility in Faribault, Minnesota. Sergeant Dunnom was working with ATF personnel from Washington, D.C.

On Tuesday evening, the lead story on the ten o'clock news began, "Officer down, but wait 'til we tell you what kind of officer it was. I'll be back with details." And then there were seemingly endless commercials. At last, the announcer came back, "A fleeing drug suspect ran from his car after speeding from St. Paul and crashing into an S.U.V. near the corner of Chicago and East Minnehaha Parkway in Minneapolis. Robert Edwards and his canine partner, Rico, gave chase on foot. Gun shots were exchanged." More details came the next day. Officer Edwards knew that the man was armed and dangerous. The man continued to run after being warned to stop. When Edwards released Rico, the man continued to shoot at Edwards, who lacked cover but was able to continue his pursuit along a hedgerow. When he moved from behind the hedge, he saw

Painted on the classroom wall of the Timothy J. Jones Training Facility is the unit's logo. Courtesy of the author.

Rico demonstrates his agility with his partner, Robert Edwards, on graduation day, May 25, 2006. Courtesy of the St. Paul Pioneer Press, *Craig Borck, photographer.*

that Rico had made the struggling suspect drop his gun and had him firmly on the ground. Other officers were then able to make the arrest. When Rico was told to release his grip, Edwards discovered that a bullet had gone through Rico's paw. Rico was taken for emergency treatment. Other officers found more ammunition as well as methamphetamine in the man's truck.

When Sergeant Dunnom was interviewed the next morning, he said, "Rico's performance was outstanding. I think he performed exactly as we train them to." Thursday morning's *St. Paul Pioneer Press* headline read, "Wounded police dog home, on the mend." The article went on to say that the University of Minnesota Veterinary Medical Center would treat Rico every day for a week to prevent infection. Meanwhile Rico was to be on kennel rest at home with his family, who would be giving him some well-deserved TLC.

In recognition of Rico's valiant service, Wal-Mart sent a $2,000 donation to the St. Paul Police K-9 Foundation and a foot-long bone to Rico. He returned to work fully healed a month later. In March 2008, Edwards and Rico were named USPCA Canine Team of the Year, competing with nominations from North America.

The Sergeant also schedules events that interface with the public. Several years ago both handlers and dogs gave many hours to the production of an *Animal Planet* episode on television. Demonstrations at the Minnesota State Fair and countless other public events are arranged on a regular basis. College students come to learn about the work of the unit for special reports, usually for college newspapers. It is often difficult to balance the time for public requests with the regular work of the unit.

The cost of having a police canine unit is considerable, especially the start-up costs. Some towns call canine police "non-essential," although that attitude is less common because it has been well documented that a properly trained police dog gives law enforcement officers one of the finest, non-lethal aides in the prevention and detection of crime. Some towns and cities want to have one or two canine police teams, but there are no public funds available for purchase of a dog, training, and other expenses required for a canine team. Nonetheless, some communities find ways to raise private money for a canine program. For example, the Safety Board of the Twin Cities suburb of Woodbury recently held a dinner in order to raise money for two police dogs. Washburn County in Wisconsin has had a canine program since 1993. At this writing, they are raising money for a new dog. They will need $16,000 and they already have raised about $11,000 from six sources. They expect to reach their goal soon. In another nearby community, an individual donor purchased a dog for his police department. These are some of the ways that smaller communities deal with the issue of the direct cost of a $7,200 dog and a loss of police officer for 12 weeks of training. The Washburn County handler will be assigned to a dog from the St. Paul program and will train in St. Paul.

Public support for canine units comes in various ways. The St. Paul Unit is supported by the St. Paul Police K-9 Foundation, which began on September 21, 1994, as a K-9 Memorial Fund.

It was established by the City Council to provide the Police Department with the authority to accept donations in the memory of Officer Timothy Jones and his dog, Laser. Donations were designated for the Canine Unit. On October 5, 1994, that memorial fund became the St. Paul Police K-9 Foundation, which was then incorporated and received its charter from the State of Minnesota. The first Board of Directors included Dr. David Wetherill, Kathy Wetherill, Cindy Carlson, James Cox, and Lt. Don Pazdernik.

Since 1998, the St. Paul Police K-9 Foundation has grown and continues to do so. The Foundation Web site states their mission: "The St. Paul Police K-9 Foundation is a tax-exempt nonprofit corporation organized exclusively for educational and charitable purposes. Its mission is to provide financial support for the St. Paul Police Canine Unit." The Foundation provides individuals and corporations the opportunity to support law enforcement by making tax-deductible donations and it promotes positive relations between the Canine Unit and area businesses, organizations, and individuals. While entirely independent of the City of St. Paul Police Department, the St. Paul Police K-9 Foundation collaborates with the Canine Unit to identify and prioritize special needs that are not funded through the City of St. Paul's ordinary budgeting process.

In the last 12 years, the Foundation has been able to aid the unit in many ways. Funds raised have paid for a large classroom, two offices, a rest room, and a coffee room for their small training center building. Other financial support enabled the unit to construct a new storage building, add a concrete patio and sidewalk around the building, and add field lighting. The Foundation paid for two new sets of agility equipment for training and demonstrations, graded the training field for better drainage, installed an irrigation system, and installed fencing around the training field. They purchased a laser gun for exclusive use of the K-9 Unit and provided ballistic helmets and body armor for all K-9 handlers.

The Foundation is particularly interested in helping first-time canine units. It is estimated that the initial start-up cost of a unit is $30,000. This includes the cost of the dog, the cost of the training, the cost of a kennel and a special squad car, and the cost of having the officer gone for the twelve weeks of training. The Foundation offers a $4,000 matching grant to communities. The community must raise $4,000 from local citizens and organizations. This covers the purchase of a $7,200 dog and the cost of the training. The Foundation pays the City of St. Paul $2,500 for the cost of the training. This arrangement may be made for a second dog also. The Foundation has purchased imported K-9s since the year 2000. Currently, they use two vendors for the purchase of six dogs each year, two for St. Paul and four for outside canine units. The vendor pre-screens the dogs' health, temperament, and suitability for canine work. An anonymous donor has made a long-term commitment to provide matching funds for the purchase of dogs.

For communities that have ongoing programs, the local unit buys the dog directly from a vendor and pays the city for the training. There are several other canine training centers in the state, but many canine units prefer to have their dogs and handlers trained in St. Paul. In fact, St. Paul has trained over 200 teams, mainly from Minnesota, Wisconsin, Iowa, and North Dakota.

The Foundation pays $8,000 to $9,000 each year to send five St. Paul teams to the U.S. Police Canine Association National Field Trials. The success of these teams, both individually and collectively, is discussed in Chapter Seven.

In July 2007, the Foundation purchased a 2004 Ford E350 van. It will be used to transport dogs that arrive from out-of-state. Some dogs flown from Europe arrive in Chicago. The van can pick up the dogs in Chicago, which saves shipping costs and perhaps saves some anxiety on the part of the dogs. The van is also used to carry merchandise that is sold at the State Fair and other venues.

Larry Kelly, retired Vice President of Field Operations at Kraus-Anderson Construction Company, has been President of the Foundation since 1997. The current board members are listed in Appendix B. Currently the St. Paul Police K-9 Foundation has assets of over $100,000.

There are many reasons that the St. Paul Police Canine Unit is so outstanding. One is that they are part of an excellent Police Department. Secondly, they are members of the U.S. Police Canine Association, the professional organization that certifies the quality of performance of its member canine teams. Every year, as noted previously, each team goes to a regional meeting for re-certification by nationally certified judges. The City of St. Paul pays for this because they know the importance of having the highest quality services for the community and its citizens. Many cities do not belong to this organization and therefore their teams are never evaluated by outside experts.

Another reason for the unit's success is their excellent working relationships with the St. Paul Police Department members who use their services. Comments by these officers are complimentary and sometimes amusing. The following remarks come from a sample of their comments. "The K-9 presence is huge." "K-9 cops are great to work with. They are high performance, smart cops before they ever become doggers." "Sometimes I can identify the handler by looking at the dog. They take on the same mannerisms." "It is always comforting to know that a K-9 is nearby." "The unit is greatly respected."

Having achieved a local, national, and international reputation for high performance standards at work and continued high performance in national competitions, the unit has other goals. They wish to continue to search for even better dogs and better ways of training. They wish to continue to serve as a model for others to emulate and be a resource for new and small units while continuing to learn themselves. The handlers are modest about their achievements as they go about their jobs courageously each day in St. Paul. More than one officer has said that pride and professionalism are the driving forces that make this an outstanding Police Canine Unit.

Executive Officers and Head Trainers: 1972-2008

Executive Officers

Sergeant Paul Dunnom, 2005–present

Sergeant Paul Rhodes, 1997–2005

Sergeant Joseph Renteria, 1992–1997

Sergeant Thomas Foss, 1989–1991

Sergeant Thomas Burke, 1973–1989

Head Trainers

Mark Ficcadenti, 1999 to present

Donald Slavik, 1997–1999

Paul Rhodes, 1996–1997

James Long, 1980–1996

James Cocchiarella, 1975–1980

2008 Members
of the St. Paul K-9 Police
Foundation Board

☆ Chair, Lawrence M. Kelly, Stillwater, MN ☆

☆ Jerry Romero, St. Paul, MN ☆

☆ Norm Carlson, Chisago City, MN ☆

☆ Stephen Boerboon, Prior Lake, MN ☆

☆ Jack Schletty, West St. Paul, MN ☆

☆ John Ballis, White Bear Lake, MN ☆

☆ Jane Tschida, Pine City, MN ☆

☆ Randy Sparling, Burnsville, MN ☆

☆ Michael Walsh, Osceola, WI ☆

2008 Officers
of the St. Paul Police
Historical Society Board

★ Retired Deputy Chief Ed Steenberg, President ★

★ Retired Senior Commander Laurence McDonald, Vice President ★

★ Kate Cavett, Secretary ★

★ Retired Sergeant Dave Hubenette, Treasurer ★

★ Sergeant Kevin Reinke, Departmental Historian ★

★ Officer Tim Bradley, Sergeant-at-Arms ★

★ Chief John Harrington, Ex-Officio ★

The 2008
St. Paul Police
Canine Unit

Handler	Dog	Handler	Dog
Sergeant Paul Dunnom	Sue	Mike McAlpine	Deuce
Mark Blumberg	Cobra	Pat Murphy	Boomer
Jason Brodt	Nitro	Jim Nash	Bingo
John Buchmeier	Andy	Dave Pavlak	Chico
Mike Davis	Auggie	Nicole Rasmussen	Chase
Bob Edwards	Rico	Pete Renteria	Lance
Mike Ernster	Buzz	Isaac Rhinehart	Sarik
Mark Ficcadenti	Shadow	Jeremy Ryan	Ranger
Brady Harrison	Sully	Jon Sherwood	Benji
Nick Kellum	Juda	Jay Thompson	Harley
Dave Longbehn	Kody	Rob Vetsch	Charlie

Chapter One The History of Using Dogs in Police Work

Allred, Alexandra Powe. *Dogs' Most Wanted: The Top 10 Book of Historic Hounds, Professional Pooches and Canine Oddities.* Washington, D.C.: Alfred Brassey's, Inc., 2004.

Bauer, Nona Kilgore. *Dog Heroes of September 11th.* Allenhurst, NJ: Kennel Club Books, 2006.

Best, Joel G. *Police Work in the Nineteenth Century City: Arrest Practices in St. Paul, 1869-1874.* Master's thesis, University of Minnesota, 1979.

Chapman, Samuel G. *Police Dogs in North America.* Springfield, IL: Charles Thomas, 1990.

Holman, Arthur. *My Dog Rex.* New York: Funk, 1958.

Orbaan, Albert. *Dogs Against Crime: True Accounts of Canine Training and Exploits in Worldwide Police Work, Past and Present.* New York: The John Day Company, 1965.

Ross, John and Barbara McKinney. *Dog Talk: Training Your Dog Through a Canine Point of View.* New York: St. Martin's Press, 1992.

Shewmake, Tiffin. *Canine Courage: The Heroism of Dogs.* Otsego, MI: PageFree Publishing, Inc., 2002.

United States Police Canine Association, Inc., Region XVIII. *History of the U.S. Police Canine Association.* Undated.

Chapter Two The First Use of Police Dogs in St. Paul

Best, Joel. *Police Work in the Nineteenth Century City: Arrest Practices in St. Paul, 1869-1874.* Master's thesis, University of Minnesota, 1979.

Best, Joel. "Keeping the Peace in St. Paul." *Minnesota History* (Summer 1981), 240-248.

Boxmeyer, Don. "St. Paul Cops Save their Past." *St. Paul Pioneer Press* (December 7, 2007), B1.

Buehlman, Ed. Interview with author, October 17, 2007.

Cavett, Kate. *"Commander Laurence Francis McDonald."* Oral History. St. Paul, MN: HAND in HAND Productions, 2005 and 2006.

Cavett, Kate. *"Those Were the Things That Went On in the St. Paul Police Department."* Oral History. St. Paul, MN: HAND in HAND Productions, St. Paul, 2004.

Chapman, Samuel G. *Police Dogs in North America.* Springfield, IL: Charles Thomas, 1990.

Kaphingst, Fred. *The Early History of the St. Paul Police Department.* St. Paul, MN: St. Paul Police Department, 1988.

Kusch, Frank. *Battleground Chicago: The Police and the 1968 Democratic National Convention.* Westport, CT: Praeger Publishers, 2004.

Maccabee, Paul. *John Dillinger Slept Here: A Crook's Tour of Crime and Corruption in St. Paul, 1920–1936.* St. Paul, MN: Minnesota Historical Society Press, 1995.

McDonald, Laurence. Interviews with author, October 17, 2007 and November 5, 2007.

United States Police Canine Association, Inc. *Fourteenth Annual Dog Trials and Seminar: St. Paul, Minnesota, August Sixth to the Tenth, 1979.* Program.

Wangstad, Wayne. "W. Swiger, Retired Police Officer Dies." *St. Paul Pioneer Press* (December 23, 1993), 6B.

———— *The Long Blue Line History*. St. Paul, MN: St. Paul Police Department, 1984. Coordinated by Cindy Mullan.

———— *St. Paul Police Department: A Historical Review 1854-2000*. Paducah, KY: Turner Publishing Co., 2000.

Chapter Three Police Dogs Return to St. Paul

Chapman, Samuel G. *Police Dogs in North America*. Springfield, IL: Charles Thomas, 1990.

Cocchiarella, James. Interview with author, November 21, 2007.

Derr, Mark. *Dog's Best Friend*. New York: Henry Holt and Company, 1997.

Ficcadenti, Mark. Interview with author, November 15, 2007.

"K-9 Unit Additions." *S.P.P.D. Report*, 1:2, May 1973.

Kothe, Glen. Interview with author, October 30, 2007; telephone interview, November 13, 2007.

Lynaugh, Tim. Interview with author, November 19, 2007.

Nevin, Larry. Interviews with author, November 20, 2007 and December 4, 2007.

Shefchik, Rick. "Champion K-9 Unit reels with transfers, resignation." *St. Paul Pioneer Press* (February 4, 1996), 1A.

Shields, Mark and Dan Glass. "What the Skills Course is About." *Minnesota Police Journal* (February 1982).

Slavik, Donald. Telephone interview with author, November 1, 2007.

Smith, Archie. Interview with author, November 21, 2007; telephone interview, November 23, 2007.

St. Paul Police Historical Society Web site: www.spphs.org/history.

———— "Police Agencies may owe back pay for 'Dog Time.'" *St. Paul Pioneer Press* (January 22, 1990), 4B.

———— *St. Paul Police Department: A Historical Review 1854-2000*. Paducah, KY: Turner Publishing Co., 2000.

Chapter Four Education and Training of Handlers

Ficcadenti, Mark. Interviews with author, November 15, December 5, and December 19, 2007.

Gottfried, Mara H. "45 new cops wear the badge." *St. Paul Pioneer Press* (December 21, 2007), B1.

Gottfried, Mara H. "Exhausted and exhilarated." *St. Paul Pioneer Press* (October 8, 2007), B1.

Griffin, James S. "Blacks in the St. Paul Police Department, an Eight-Year Survey." *Minnesota History* (Fall, 1975), 255-265.

Griffin, James S. *Blacks in the St. Paul Police and Fire Departments 1885–1976*. St. Paul, MN: E & J, Inc., 1978.

Home Office Standing Advisory Committee on Police Dogs. *Northumbria Police Dogs, Training and Care*. 1996.

Milani, Myrna. *The Body Language and Emotions of Dogs*. Wm. Morrow & Co., 1988.

Myers, John. "When Duty Calls, They Answer: German Shepherds Newest K-9 Partners." *St. Paul Pioneer Press* (June 20, 1999), 14C.

St. Paul Police Department. *Canine Training Manual*. 1997.

Chapter Five The Remarkable Dogs

Bureau of Police, St. Paul, Minnesota. "The Use of Dogs in Police Work." *Training Bulletin*, February 18, 1959.

Coren, Stanley. *The Intelligence of Dogs*. New York: Free Press, 2006.

Ficcadenti, Mark. Interview with author, January 9, 2008.

Gardner, Bill. "Cop dog dies in 'work he loved.'" *St. Paul Pioneer Press* (May 20, 1982), B1.

Keating, Trish. *The Special One: The Story of a Police Dog*. St. Paul, MN: Shamrock Publishing, 1994.

United States Police Canine Association, Inc. *Fourteenth Annual Dog Trials and Seminar, August Sixth to the Tenth, 1979*. Program.

Chapter Six Officer Down

Briggs, Gary. "The Best of Us All." *Minnesota Police Journal* (October 1994), 10-11, 20.

Chin, Richard and Tim Nelson. "Suspect Caught After Intense Manhunt." *St Paul Pioneer Press* (August 27, 1994), 1A, 7A.

Gottried, Mara H. "The Darkest Day." *St. Paul Pioneer Press* (August 22, 2004), 1A.

Lanpher, Katherine. "Rites to Have Bright and Shining Moment." *St. Paul Pioneer Press* (August 31, 1994), 1A.

Larose, Sherri. "Fallen Officers Remembered." *St. Paul Pioneer Press* (August 22, 2004), 1A.

Lednicer, Lisa Grace. "Thousands Bid Sad Farewell/Dazed St. Paul Mourns Ryan on Longest Day." *St. Paul Pioneer Press* (August 31, 2004), 1A.

Livingston, Nancy and Theresa Monsour. "Off-Duty Officer Volunteered to Search for Comrade's Killer." *St Paul Pioneer Press* (August 27, 1994), 5A.

Morrison, Blake. "Officers, Public Mourn Tim Jones." *St. Paul Pioneer Press* (August 29, 1994), 1A.

Nelson, Tim. "Chronicle of Two Killings/Baker Says He would Have Shot More Men if He'd Had the Means." *St. Paul Pioneer Press* (August 30, 1994), 1A.

Nelson, Tim. "Shooting Suspect Admits to Killing St. Paul Officers." *St. Paul Pioneer Press* (August 28, 1994), 1A.

Rosario, Rubén. "Account of Shootings Still Chills." *St. Paul Pioneer Press* (August 23, 2004), 1A.

Von Kreisler, Kristin. *The Compassion of Animals*. Rocklin, CA: Prima Publishing, 1997.

———"Calm Morning Turns Into Day of Grieving." *St. Paul Pioneer Press* (August 27, 1994), 1A.

———"Funeral Notices for Tim Jones and Ron Ryan, Jr." *St. Paul Pioneer Press* (August 29, 1994), 6D.

Chapter Seven Recognition and Awards

Adelmann, Paul. "St. Paul Police Department Wins Top Team Canine Honors." *Minnesota Police Journal*, (December 1989), 7.

Case Reports sent to USPCA from 1998–2008.

Cocchiarella, James. "Officer Klinge and K-9 Radar." *Canine Courier* (April 1979).

Holtz, Doug. "Saint Paul Police Duo Win National K-9 Championship." *Minnesota Police Journal* (December 1998), 17.

Pavlak, David. Interview with author, January 10, 2008.

Pazdernik, Lt. Donald and Officer Donald Slavik. "St. Paul Canine Unit Earns Top Honors." *Minnesota Police Journal* (December 1995), 4-7.

——— *St. Paul Police Department: A Historical Review 1854-2000*. Paducah, KY: Turner Publishing Co., 2000.

Chapter Eight The St. Paul Police Canine Unit Today

Dunnom, Sergeant Paul. Interview with author, November 13, 2007.

Gottfried, Mara H. "Industry Magazine names cop, police dog 'Team of the year.'" *St. Paul Pioneer Press* (April 2, 2008), 6B.

Gottfried, Mara H. "Wounded police dog home, on the mend." *St. Paul Pioneer Press* (October 11, 2007), 1B.

Kelly, Lawrence M. Interview with author, October 15, 2007, and e-mail, December 19, 2007.

Rasmussen, Nicole. Interview with author, November 15, 2007.

Shaw, Bob. "They fight crime, but not for free." *St. Paul Pioneer Press* (September 9, 2007), B1.

St. Paul Police K-9 Foundation Web site: www.stpaulpolicek-9foundation.com.

Thornley, Bill. "Washburn County Seeks New K-9 Officer." *Spooner Advocate*, September 20, 2007.

Vezner, Tad. "Drug suspect nabbed after chase, shootout." *St. Paul Pioneer Press* (October 10, 2007), 1A.

———"Kids Raise $360 for Dog." *St. Paul Pioneer Press* (October 8, 1994), 2D.

Anderson, Terry 52

Baker, Guy Harvey 57, 58, 62, 63
Bergren, Tom 61
Blumberg, Mark 72, 73
Boll, Dave 32, 65, 67, 68, 70
Brodt, Jason 71, 72, 76
Buchmeier, John 71, 72
Buehlman, Ed 16, 18, 19, 22, 23
Bulver, Donald 28, 70
Burke, Eugene 51, 70, 72
Burke, Thomas 30, 51

C.I.R.T. (Critical Incident Response Team) 59, 71
Cocchiarella, James 26, 27, 46
Cupperas 1, 2

Davis, Mike 72, 76
DNR (Department of Natural Resources) 42
Dog programs, attitudes towards 6
DOGNY 7, 8
Dogs, breeds used 7, 9, 16, 42, 45
Dogs, cemeteries for 52-54, 61
Dogs, competitions of 60, 61, 65-68
Dogs, crime solvers 1-5
Dogs, health of 50
Dogs, killed in action 50-55
Dogs, psychology and training 6
Dogs, quality assessment of 46, 49
Dogs, selection of 7, 9, 76
Dogs, source of 46
Dogs, temperament of 45, 46
Dogs, training centers 31, 33
Dogs, training programs 3-6, 30, 31, 33, 42, 46-
    50, 76
Dox 4, 5
Dunnom, Paul 41, 70, 75, 76, 79

Edwards, Robert 76-79

Ficcadenti, Dan 36, 37
Ficcadenti, Mark 36-39, 41, 45, 65, 71, 76, 77
Finney, Chief William 32, 58, 59
Fisher, Michael 27, 28

Garvey, Russ 61, 65, 67, 68
Geyer, Chuck 72
Griffin, Deputy Chief James 36

Handlers, selection of 9, 32, 37, 38, 76
Handlers, training of 27, 28, 35-43
Hansen, Richard 42
Harrison, Brady 71
Hercules 2

Johnson, Al 16
Jones, Timothy 51, 52, 57-63, 65, 68, 69

Kaase, Ed 17
Kangas, Dale 72
Kellum, Nick 73
Kelly, Larry 52, 81
King Memorial Award 68
Klinge, Mark 30, 50-51, 68
Kothe, Glen 25-29, 31, 47

Law Enforcement Assistance Act 35
Long, James 30-32, 65
Lynaugh, Josh 36
Lynaugh, Timothy 36, 42, 51, 52, 70
Lyttle, Pat 61, 65, 66

Majors, Greg 65, 66
Martin, Donald 28, 50
McAdams, Donald 30
McAuliffe, Chief Lester 22
McCutcheon, Deputy Chief William 27, 32, 72
McDonald, Laurence 15-18, 21-23, 69, 70
Minnesota Peace Officers Memorial 63

Nevin, Lawrence 26, 28, 30, 38, 42, 48, 50
Nord, Deputy Chief John C., 72

O'Brien, Mike 65
O'Connor policy 22

Pavlak, David 70, 71, 76
POST (Peace Officers Standards and Training
    Board) 35, 36
Poucher, Tim 72

Rasmussen, Nicole 40, 41
Rex III 4
Rhodes, Paul 65
Rowan, Chief Richard 27
Ryan, Ron, Jr., 51, 57-63, 69

Sackett, James 25, 26
Schultz, Bradley 70
Search and Rescue dogs 6, 7
Sherwood, Jon 45, 61, 65, 67, 68, 76
Slavik, Donald 30, 50, 70
Sletner, Mark 65
Smith, Archie 30, 31, 69
St. Paul Police Canine Unit, members 86
St. Paul Police Canine Unit, officers and trainers
    83
St. Paul Police Department, canine unit
    graduation ceremonies 41- 43
St. Paul Police Department, history of 11-15, 22,
    23, 25, 27, 31-33, 35-38, 68-73, 75, 76
St. Paul Police Department, legacy applicants 36,
    37, 75
St. Paul Police Department, medals awarded 69,
    70
St. Paul Police Department, women in 12, 15, 31,
    32, 36, 40, 41, 75
St. Paul Police Historical Society, board of 85
St. Paul Police K-9 Foundation 79-81
St. Paul Police K-9 Foundation, board of 84
Swiger, Bill 14, 16, 18, 21, 23

Timothy J. Jones Training Facility 33, 41, 42, 63,
    73, 77

USPCA (United States Police Canine
    Association) 7, 65-70, 79, 81
Ulysses 2, 3

Wiegel, Mark 33
William O. Stillman Award 68